KING SOLOMON SPIRITUAL LIBRARY
THE GOD ENCYCLOPAEDIA WORD OF INFINITY

BY
THE SPIRIT OF THE FATHER GOD
THROUGH HIS SERVANT
HRM KING SOLOMON DAVID JESSE ETE
(King Solomon Spiritual Library)
Eteroyal Universal Family BCS

The book cover picture is copyright to Solomon ETE

This book is published by
King Solomon Spiritual Library
P O BOX 27394
London E12 6WW UK
www.kingsolomonspirituallibrary.com

A CIP record for this book is available from the British Library

ISBN 978-0-9561498-0-0

F: WHEN I BROKE THE EGG OF LIFE, THE SPOKEN WORD, IT WAS IN AFRICA

G: WHEN I MOULDED THE FIRST MAN IN MY HAND, IT WAS IN AFRICA

CONCLUSION A:
AFRICA THE MOTHER AND FATHER'S LAND

CONCLUSION B:
AFRICA, THE CENTRE OF THE FIRST SCHOOL GROUND

CONCLUSION C:
AFRICA IS ALPHA AND OMEGA, ADAM AND OLUMBA, EVE AND OBU

INTRODUCTION
A: AFRICA, THE FOCUS POINT

B: WHY ARE AFRICANS BACKWARD?

C: THE FIRST THING IS ALONE

D: THE DOWNFALL OF AFRICA IS SIN

E: THE FIRST SHALL BE THE LAST

F: HE WHO LAUGHS AT THE LAST HAS THE BEST LAUGHTER

G: AFRICA IS THE FATHER GOD

CONCLUSION A: AFRICA, THE SOURCE AND THE DESTINATION

CONCLUSION B: AFRICA IS THE MAKER OF MAKERS

CONCLUSION C: YOU MUST LOVE TO UNDERSTAND THIS WORD

PART THREE   *99-130*

INTRODUCTION:

A: NIGERIA IS WHERE RIVER NIGER IS IN THE MIDDLE OF THE CITY EARTH

B: THE UNIVERSAL SUPREME MYSTERY IS THE COUNTRY OF NIGERIA

C: THE NIGERIA IS IN AFRICA, THE FATHER GOD'S PLACE OF BIRTH

D: NIGERIA IS WHERE ABEL SHOWED HIS FIRST APPRECIATION TO GOD

E: HALLE-SELASSIEI WAS ANOTHER TRANSIT OF ABEL WHICH IS THE SAME KING SOLOMON.

F: ETHIOPIA SHALL ARISE

G: THE NIGERIA IN THE AFRICA WELCOMES THE HOLY SPIRIT OF TRUTH PERSONIFIED

CONCLUSION A:
OLUMBA OLUMBA OBU, THE FINAL WORD IN PERSON, THE FINAL PHYSICAL HOUSE OF THE SUPREME WORD

CONCLUSION B:
IT IS ONLY EVIL THAT HATES WHAT IS GOOD AND ONLY SATAN THAT DENIES THE TRUTH

CONCLUSION C:
THE TRUTH IS AN UNCHANGEABLE PHENOMENON

C: THE WORD SEASON CELEBRATION

D: WITH LOVE

E: READ SEVEN LECTURES

F: INVITATION

G: THE TITLE LIST OF THE FATHER'S TALK

Part One

THE
NIGERIA
IN
THE
AFRICA

THE CYCLE OF CONCLUSION

=============

AFRICA,
THE FATHER'S
LAND

FATHER'S TALK

(GOD PRESENT)

Date: AO/OC/OH (The tenth day of the third month of **THE FATHER**, year two thousand and eight).

In the name of **OUR LORD JESUS CHRIST**, In the blood of **OUR LORD** Jesus **CHRIST** Now ever and forever more, *Amien*.

Today, it pleases **ME THE FATHER GOD THE CREATOR OF THE UNIVERSE** to give this Lecture Revelation based on **NIGERIA** with the title, **THE NIGERIA IN THE AFRICA**. And part 'A' of this Lecture Revelation is **AFRICA, THE FATHER'S LAND**.

A: **INTRODUCTION**

Through the will of **THE FATHER GOD**, I always talk to all the **FATHER'S TALK** readers and all children of **GOD** who like the **TRUTH** and are eager and hungry for the **TRUTH**. As it is often said, the **TRUTH** shall set you **FREE** and this is the time that the **TRUTH** has come to set everyone **FREE**. Every soul that wants and likes, and accepts the **TRUTH** must be **FREE**. They must have the **TOTAL FREEDOM** from **THE FATHER GOD** and, **HAPPINESS** and **JOY** from the **HOLY SPIRIT OF TRUTH**. Humankind was created through the **SPIRIT OF TRUTH** and I **THE CREATOR OF THE UNIVERSE** is that **TRUTH**. The only thing that is unchangeable and cannot be deceived and bribed is the **TRUTH** and that **TRUTH** is the **SPOKEN WORD** which is I, **THE FATHER GOD** with everything put together about **ME.** This Revelation

Lecture does not come from man; it comes from **THE FATHER GOD HIMSELF** and **THE FATHER GOD** means **SOMETHING** which **ALREADY EXISTS** from the time of existence for eternity.

There is no mouth that can explain and expatiate on the meaning of **THE FATHER GOD**. The only way that you will know **THE FATHER GOD** is for you to live by the **TRUTH** and believe the **WORD** of **TRUTH** and also stand with the **WORD** of **TRUTH**. It is either through what you think or through what you hear via someone else. If the **WORD** is based on the **TRUTH** then it means that, it is **GOD** but if it is based on falsehood then it is negative and satanic. This is why two things are ruling the world through one phenomenon as **ONE THING** that has split into two as **POSITIVE** and negative because of the **WORD**. When you go through King Solomon Spiritual Library, where information about **GOD** is now revealed as the mind of **GOD**, then you will understand that the tree in the middle of the Garden of Eden is the **WORD** that has two branches as **POSITIVE** and negative. Today, I want to reveal the first part of the secret of the world that I promised to reveal which will start in this Lecture Revelation. The introduction of this Lecture Revelation is for you to tune yourself to **GOD** which means **LOVE**, **HUMILITY** and a **PEACEFUL** heart. I know that some humans do not like to hear anything in the name of 'something' and if they come across it, they will throw it away. They are not interested when they hear of something that is not from their usual source. Some people do not read other peoples **WORD** but the **WORD** is **GOD**. They only concentrate on what they already know but how do you know that your capacity is enough to save you or to give you enough understanding from the information at hand. If you are **POSITIVE**, listen to **POSITIVE WORD**. You will know any **WORD** that is **POSITIVE** via your conscience if you are correct. Take some time to go through a few of **FATHER'S TALK** in King Spiritual Solomon Library which **I** have now brought back to the earth. If you go through one or two Lecture Revelations and you think that it is the **WORD** of a human being then your heart is not clear and you have evil spirit in you. However, if your heart is clear and you have **LOVE** and come from **THE FATHER GOD** and believe in **THE FATHER GOD** then by the time that you read one Lecture Revelation, you will have something that will elevate your soul. This only works through **HUMILITY** and a **PEACEFUL** heart which are in unity of your mind with **ONENESS** of heart that will give you the higher consciousness to come closer to **GOD**.

A: AFRICA THE FATHER'S LAND

What is the meaning of **AFRICA**? **AFRICA** literally means the **FIRST** as the centre of the **FIRST** point. **AFRICA** actually means **ALPHA** and the name sake of the first man, Adam.

Adam means the first thing as number one. And number one means alone therefore, **AFRICA** means alone, a place that is alone as **ALPHA** the first thing. **AFRICA** means **THE FATHER ALONE EXIST FROM THE BEGINNING OF TIME** and I named **AFRICA MYSELF** in the physical reality as **ALPHA**, number one, the first thing that is alone and that is Adam. The first **WORD** that manifests in human form was Adam as the first home. The spot where I created the first man in **MY** hand is the meaning of **AFRICA** as **THE FATHER'S LAND**. I know that in the past, no one took **AFRICA** seriously and that is how it is. From today, through this Revelation Lecture, you will know why you do not take **AFRICA** seriously. And even those in **AFRICA** do not take themselves seriously but that time has passed because today is a **NEW BREATHE** from a **NEW SPIRIT** and the **NEW CREATION** for **AFRICA**. And that is why the revelation of **GOD** today is based on **AFRICA**.

B: **AFRICA, THE CYCLE OF CONCLUSION**

AFRICA is the **CYCLE OF CONCLUSION** because it is where everything eminent from. This Lecture Revelation would not be too lengthy but it is an eye opener to every human being including those that would be born in a hundred plus years to come. This is an everlasting record and an everlasting testimony and everlasting revelation that have never happened before. **I** now want to call the spade, the spade and by so doing arrange things well in the whole world so that everyone should respect and value each other. This is important because you cannot **VALUE** what you do not **KNOW**. People do not **VALUE AFRICA** because they do not know what **AFRICA** is and **AFRICANS** do not **VALUE** themselves because they do not know who they are and the land on which they dwell. They do not know what is in the land. **AFRICA** is the father and mother of all human beings. **AFRICA** is where the egg of nature broke before the nature took place. I **AM** the only **ONE** that knows the secret of **MY** Kingdom and that is what I have exposed now to humankind since the **HOLY SPIRIT** is the last **PERSONIFIED** entity. And it is because of this that I have to bring every secret and every revelation so that humankind would know how to treat their life. **AFRICA IS THE CYCLE**

OF CONCLUSION because everything ends where it starts. That is why you must fear a cycle ring and what a ring means. All the old masters and rebellious angels that have established secret societies know the meaning of a ring. A ring is something that is round and when something circles around you then you are in, as included, therefore, every human being on earth comes from **AFRICA**. Whether you are a solid thick skinned person or soft and lighter skinned person and any other or short, tall, big or small or of any other form, you come from **AFRICA**. Everything of everything comes from **AFRICA**. **AFRICA** means the **WORD** and that is why **AFRICA** is the father. All scientists that do research in this area have discovered this but they refuse to expose it because they are not **TRUTHFUL**. People hide all the **POSITIVE** and **PROMOTIONAL** things that they have discovered about

AFRICA because they are jealous and evil. It is only **THE FATHER GOD** that can expose all **TRUTHS**. Some people would have a dream about someone but they will never tell the person about the dream because they are jealous. This is what happened to Ruben and his brothers. They had a dream about Joseph, their youngest brother that showed that they would all bow down to him but because of jealousy they never told him. They hid it but it did not matter. At the end of the day, the **TRUTH** always comes to past. And because they hid the **TRUTH** from Joseph, they suffered for forty years in slavery. And it is for hiding the **TRUTH** that the whole world are suffering and having so many problems everywhere. I, **THE FATHER GOD THE CREATOR OF THE UNIVERSE** have revealed so many things to humans but no one has brought these things out in the **TRUTHFUL** way? Scientist have looked in so many places and discovered things in the sky, in the stars and in many other places but they hide the **TRUTH** and because of hiding the **TRUTH**, the pending doom is following them in the whole world. And that is why **I** have no alternative than to come by **MYSELF** and expose the **TRUTH** so that children of **GOD** will be **FREE**. If for instance you dream that your son is your grandfather or your daughter is your mother or grandmother and you refuse to act on it, then you will suffer for it. If **GOD** reveals anything for you as the **TRUTH** and you hide it because it does not favour you in your thinking, you will suffer for it.

Today **I AM** releasing and setting **FREE** all human beings by bringing this Revelation Lecture so that they will respect, worship and honour their **FATHER GOD** in **AFRICA**. Everybody's father is **AFRICA** and as a result, the whole world should worship **AFRICA**. And they must **RESPECT** and **LOVE AFRICA** and support **AFRICA** because that is where your soul lives. The soul of everyone comes from **AFRICA**. You can only be sent out to other places on transit or on mission of work to spread the **WORD** of **GOD** that should lavishly cover the earth but the soul of every creation emanates from **THE FATHER GOD** which **I** established. And **HIS** home as the **EXISTENCE** is in **AFRICA**. That is why **AFRICA IS THE CYCLE OF CONCLUSION**.

C: **THE FATHER IS THE SOURCE AND THE DESTINATION**

This is **AFRICA**. What **I** mean by father is anything that that nothing else exist, before it exist. A senior person among everybody is the father of the land. Do not take a small child and call him father. A small child can be a father in spirit but in the physical world, every human being should worship and respect the older members of the family. That is the father in nature as oldness. Your soul is as old as your physical age because every child that dies young comes back with a different character but if someone dies in old age; they come back as a mature child. And that is why I give this Lecture Revelation because the whole world suffers untold hardship by knocking the head of their father, by exposing the nakedness of their father and thereby disgracing their father. Whomever that disgraces their father and mother shall die. That is why you see that people are dieing anyhow with so many problems everywhere. There are so many places in the western world that have a lot of money and have all the physical amenities in their hand to make life comfortable however, they continue to die and suffer, why? What does soft skinned fair man not have in terms of material benefits? Look at China, they have created and advanced in numerous numbers of technological products but they have all sorts of problems and are not in **PEACE**. America has untold amounts of money, in fact the synagogue of money is in America but they continue to have problems. The majority of gold is stored away in Britain and that is why they are the most valuable country presently in terms of material wealth but they have serious problems. Everywhere in the world, there are problems. The Arab worlds are blessed people but they have many problems. Do you see any **PEACE** in this world? Go to Jerusalem and you find that they are fighting and killing every second. The burner of evil is burning them because they have disgraced their father by exposing his nakedness.

All those who have stolen from **AFRICA** to enrich their country are in trouble. All the people that use cunning and craftiness to steal from **AFRICANS** and also **AFRICANS** who craftily steal from **AFRICA** are betrayers and they have everlasting problems.

I AM bringing this Lecture Revelation to save everyone. Any human being that treats **AFRICA** badly by craftily stealing from there and practicing other negative deeds that disrespect **AFRICA** in anyway are in prison in spirit. This is because **AFRICA** is the father and that is where your soul hides and projects you to anywhere and that is why you must link back to **AFRICA** now! This is the time of harvest, the universal final harvest, and every soul must link back to **AFRICA**. **AFRICA** is the father representing **THE FATHER GOD THE CREATOR OF THE UNIVERSE** where the first sound of the **WORD** came out.

It is where **I** sat down to create the entire creation and that is **HE** is **THE FATHER** and **AFRICA IS THE FATHER'S LAND** as **THE FATHER'S** place as the **SOURCE** and the **DESTINATION**. You will come from there and go back there and that is why you link back into the **CYCLE** as the **CYCLE** of the **CONCLUSION** of your soul. **I** do not say this **WORD** to please you or so that you will donate or recognize **ME**. This is the **WORD** of **TRUTH** that comes in the **SPIRIT OF TRUTH OF THE FATHER GOD** so that all **TRUE** children of **GOD** can respect themselves. If you are born in **AFRICA** and practice evil, you are an arrested person from today. And from today, this information will reach every soul in **AFRICA**. If you come from anywhere or live elsewhere to commit evil in **AFRICA**, you are in trouble and you will not have **PEACE**. You see that there are so many places in **AFRICA** that do not have **PEACE** because **AFRICAN** people are not supposed to practice evil. And you are not supposed to sit on your father's head and expose the nakedness of you father. Through this lecture, I will reveal to you why **AFRICAN** people are suffering untold hardship.

D: **WHEN I CREATED THE WORLD, I FIRST STARTED WITH AFRICA**.

When **I CREATED** the **WORLD**, I started from **AFRICA**. That is the point where the **WORD HATCHED**. When the **WORD HATCHED** from the shell, and manifested as the sound, it produced the **GEN** of **WORD** which was in **AFRICA** and when **I THE FATHER GOD** said '*LET*' be this and that, it was in **AFRICA**. That was **MY** first step and that is where I call **MY WORKSHOP**. I know that people do not respect their workshop but that is where everything lies. I do not need to talk too much about this. Check your memory and record and you will find that there is no history in this world that you can learn that is more than this. This Revelation Lecture is beyond mans prejudice and beyond the intellect of any human research, spirit or soul. This is **THE FATHER GOD'S** record. The record that is in King Solomon Spiritual Library is the first record on earth that I kept for **MYSELF** and that is why you will never hear this anywhere else in the world. When **I CREATED** the **WORLD** and everything inside, the **WORD** '*LET*' was first said in **AFRICA**, and that is where the footprint of **THE FATHER GOD** is.

E: **THE OLDEST PLACE IN THE WORLD IS AFRICA**

When I say the **OLDEST PLACE ON EARTH**, I mean the first existing land. It was twelve by twelve cubic meters around in **MY** spiritual soul. I formed **MYSELF** on top of the water and I generated **MYSELF** as a sound of glory and then I built a package to cover **MYSELF**. I then popped up the sand and left the water and separated the water from the sand. On the dry land was the egg of nature. After seven days called **SEVEN AKANSTINAS**, I hatched **MYSELF**, and when I hatched **MYSELF**, I became a moulded egg called **UNISTITS** which in **EFIK** is known as **OFUM-UWEM**. And **OFUM-UWEM** said '*LET*' be this and because of the **WORD** '*LET*' as the first **WORD**, the soul of the egg of nature that hatched **HIMSELF** as **THE FATHER GOD** was on the land of **AFRICA**. I was not White or tanned, I was **SOLID** in nature. And seventy two million colours were derived from the **SOLID** nature of the **THICK** skin. And that is why every other colour in this world can be manipulated by the solid and thick skin that you call a Black man as the completion of colour and because of that **AFRICA** is the **CYCLE OF CONCLUSION** as the **OLDEST PLACE** on the planet earth.

F: **WHEN I BROKE THE EGG OF LIFE, THE SPOKEN WORD, IT WAS IN AFRICA**

The **EGG** of **LIFE** that formed the **SPOKEN WORD** was in **AFRICA**. **AFRICA** was not a big land as it is now. Then, it was twelve by twelve cubic meters as I said earlier called **MANSTANTIN** which is to say about twelve by seventy two by twelve feet however since then I have expended this world on a second by second basis every day. I have given a revelation about how I expand the world. Sometimes I use flood, sometimes, I use earthquakes and other times, I use an in and out over flowing of water to shift the world. I have been shifting this world constantly to different angles but you will not know. The world is not a steady place, it is turning around every second, but wherever, the world moves to and comes back, the centre of the world remains as **AFRICA** and that is why any place in the world can be destroyed and anything can happen, but **AFRICA** will remain save. I can shift America, I can shift Britain and I can shift anywhere I wish. I can turn some places to the Atlantic Ocean and put the Atlantic Ocean elsewhere and do so many things to correct things using earthquakes and other means but **AFRICA** would still stand in its place. The sure foundation stone that I put in **AFRICA** would never be put anywhere else. And it is for this reason that I barrier anyone from spoiling the land of **AFRICA**. No soft skin fair person can go and manipulate the place. I have put maximum security in place to ensure this, but if not for **ME** doing this the land of **AFRICA** would have been polluted by now. All the problems in

AFRICA such as mosquitoes, the animals, the harsh sunshine, and even the character of **AFRICANS** and all the other things that people see as problematic is because of the security that I have put there so that people who are not from positive part of **ME** would run away. **AFRICA** can never be an artificial world. It is only in **AFRICA** that you are able to see that **GOD** is nature, and **GOD** is natural by making living organisms available for living creatures. In the western world, they have destroyed all the natural things. Instead, they prefer the artificial things that are evil as the plan of Satan. However, in **AFRICA**, I have put **MY** feet down to have **MY** respect. Do not bring that type of thing to **AFRICA** because, if you do, I will finish you. Do not think that you can bring technology and other forms of so called modernisation to **AFRICA** so as to spoil the natural look. When you destroy the natural look of a place, then you have destroyed the land because **I** use the tree, the water and other things to hold the foundation of the land and keep everything in place. For all the countries that have taken the natural trees away, and barrier waters from flowing freely, your land is in trouble. The earthquake will visit you because by digging the place, you have destroyed the foundation of that place. Natural disaster always fights against anything that destroys nature. If you want to build your country, you can do so without tampering with the natural design of **THE FATHER GOD** because when you do that, you destroy the land. **AFRICA**, **AFRICA** be careful and do not for any reason destroy all the natural look rather you should preserve and live with them because that is **ME THE FATHER** and **THE MOTHER GOD** in person living in you. If you destroy **ME** and put in negativity, carnality and fanciful things alone around then you are trouble. Presently, the western world does not have any good air and people are not able to breathe well. The underground is wired up to the hilt and is a fire hazard because they have destroyed the natural look and put artificial things in place. For this reason, the focus and central point of life is still in **AFRICA** because when I broke the egg of **LIFE** as the **SPOKEN WORD**, it was in **AFRICA** and that is why I have persevered **AFRICA** for the **GLORY** of **GOD**.

G: WHEN I MOULDED THE FIRST MAN IN MY HAND, IT WAS IN AFRICA

I want to correct the bad impression that scientist and evil people have created and trained people to teach the world that human beings developed from animal species because that is falsehood. I, **THE FATHER GOD**, created the real human being as Adam and Eve. When I created Adam in **MY PRESENT**, I moulded him with **MY** hand in three types of mud. I used the first mould called **MBREN** as the house and the dust put together and the second one called **NDOM** which is white chalk as the mud and then I mixed it with red mud. **MBREN** was a dark in colour and **ADUAN-NDOM** was light and fair in colour and then I used the red sand to mix them together. The **MBREN** as the dark mud represents **THE FATHER** and **NDOM** represent the **WORD** and the **RED MUD** represents the water and the blood and that is how a human being was created as image in the spiritual hospital of **GOD**. And then I breathed **MYSELF** into the moulded image that is **MY LIKENESS** as the breath of life. After that I hatched **MYSELF** as the first **WORD** and transferred **MYSELF** from the spiritual realm to the physical realm because I wanted to build a house for

MYSELF and when I did that, I called them Adam and Eve. I lived in Adam and Eve and that is the revelation that I have for you today.

CONCLUSION A:
AFRICA THE MOTHER AND FATHER'S LAND

As the above says, **AFRICA** is the land of **THE FATHER** and **THE MOTHER** in the whole world. I will reveal to you why you 'think' that you have stolen and duped **AFRICA**. Due to lack of understanding and the fact that **AFRICA** has the most resources, a lot of nations have taken from **AFRICA**. However, today I will reveal the secret that no human being has known before today. The father and the mother are the care takers of all the children. The father and the mother will suffer to have a child and take care of it by cleaning the bum when he or she soils themselves and do everything possible to ensure that they live and survive. Eventually, when the children grow and go out to establish their life, their father and mother will have become old then the reciprocation starts because they would now look after their parents through out their lives. This conduct and principle continues non stop for eternity. The father and the mother as the parents will look after their children and in turn, the children will look after their parents. And when you go and come back because you will be reversed as round **OOO**, you continue with this system. In the first **O** is the father and the mother, in the second **O** is the son as the children, and the third **O** is to come back again to be the father and that is the spirit, soul and physical as **OOO** which naturally manifest an equilibrium.

AFRICA is **THE FATHER GOD'S** land but the world has grown to have different children but as children, their land is empty. They do not have anything until they grow and become a father or mother to have a family and start to look after their children. And that is why they think that they stole things from **AFRICA** but, they did not steal anything. They took those things to go and look after themselves to grow and now that they are big and call themselves, America, Russia, India, Australia, Britain and all of Europe, China and the rest of the grown up children of the world, they have to look after **AFRICA**. Under no circumstances can they refuse to do this. If you do not do this, you are in trouble because you will not have where you will live because your soul will reverse back. The only place where people will be secure in spirit and in soul, and also in terms having sufficient food and other necessary requirements of life, is in **AFRICA**. If you do not believe, you will believe because the taste of the pudding is through eating and seeing is believing and since '**I AM THE FATHER GOD**' that is talking, I know before I talk. I talk as I know, but you refuse to hear and understand and learn as you do not know and you do not understand. **AFRICA** should forgive the whole world for stealing so much mineral resources from there. The **FATHER'S LAND** is where the treasure is, therefore those who are physically from **AFRICA** yet steal things and take the money and everything back to the western world, are not the indigenes of **AFRICA**. Let **ME** explain something to you. When the world visited the land of **AFRICA** and found that the land was rich and full with honey and milk and every other thing, they decided to find means and ways to take these things. And I sent those spirits to go on transit to lavishly establish the whole world. Now all these people have taken evolution back to **AFRICA** and have to be born as **AFRICANS,** *all nations of the world have representation in birth in* **AFRICA,** but they have no **LOVE** for the **SOLID** thick skinned people. These are the people that have evil transit that cover themselves in the **SOLID** thick skin but inside of them, they are not that. Do you believe that a **TRUE** child can steal his father's property? Do you believe that a **TRUE** wife can steal the husbands' things, when everything that your husband has is yours and everything that your father has is also yours so how do you steal these things? The son can only bring things to add so that he can enjoy it more. Equally, a husband should not steal his wife's property because what belongs to the wife is also the husband's therefore when a husband steals the wife's property and the wife steals the husband's property; they are fake husband and wife. When you see children that steal their father's property, they are fake ones. If you see a Nigerian or anyone from any **AFRICAN** country steal anything from their land to the western world, it is because they are fake Nigerians and fake **AFRICANS**. They are the counterfeit ones not the correct ones. They look like they are **SOLID** thick skinned on the body, but they are not so internally. It is only **TRUE AFRICANS** and the **TRUE** citizens that do everything to sustain their land for their father. Those who disgrace their father by exposing his nakedness are those who steal from their father and give to others in the world. It is the same evil people that have disguised themselves in different forms as helpers that tumble their governments. What makes the governments of **AFRICA** unstable and dysfunctional? It is not the government members from within the country that cause it; it is outsiders who link with evil agents to tumble the government pretending to help. Lucifer could not come straight to deceive Adam. He used serpent and serpent could not come straight to Adam, it passed through Eve and then he finally succeeded. And that is why before you see any war in **AFRICA**, it must have been instigated by an outside country and I do not want to mention their names however, those who are involved in these activities know themselves. They cannot do this to those who love their land, they can only do this to those who do not **LOVE** their land. They will say 'but do you not know that you could have been the president or the head of state of that country and so on and so forth'. 'And you could have been the king or the queen and this and that so why do you just leave things as they are'? These are the people who have established the negative democracy for evil links, some are good links, but many of them are evil links, the satanic programme that they can use to destroy good things that **GOD** has kept in place. Do you think that if this world was established by democracy, some powerful leaders of some nations would not say that they should move to **AFRICA** and let **AFRICANS** come and live in their respective countries? Because they know about the many **GOOD** things that are buried in **AFRICA**, that is the meaning of democracy, to go and demolish the original thing and superimpose with something else. When King Solomon was King James, the problem that he had was when the system of democracy was introduced. When this system was introduced, he refused it and that is where the entire problem lies. And that is how the kingdom of the United Kingdom started to spoil but King James put his feet down and said that they should not destroy the monarchy. It is only the United Kingdom that is stable in the whole world because their Monarchy is still in place. Politicians have tried to destroy the Monarchy and all the problems of the kingship are caused by politicians because those are the people that want to rule by shifting. In the morning, someone will rule and eat their portion and in the evening another person will rule and eat their portion. They are the people that share all the wealth of **GOD**. Woe into the arm robbers in disguise. And they complain that arm robbers cause problems in the land but the actual fraudulent people and arm robbers are evil politicians. Politicians are those who make laws so that they can eat and make their stomachs big whilst the actual citizens of the land are suffering. Who is supposed to be bigger and richer than another person? Did **THE FATHER GOD** create one person differently from another person? Everybody has equal right to what **GOD** has created. Why do you siphon things from one country to another leaving that country poor? And even some of the people in **AFRICA** make themselves so rich that they do not know what to do with the money but others remain pitiable. You cause woe to your soul. Any property of the government of the land is supposed to be shared equally by everyone in the land. And when you die, all the poor people that you made to suffer will haunt you. Have you ever seen any of these rich politicians and very rich people end well in their families and in their tribe? They would eventually loose everything in their soul because when you die and go you will be arrested. And that is why **I** say that **I** would make the rich to become poor and make the poor to become rich because **GOD** knows that there is no equality on earth. I have used this opportunity to reveal things for humankind and those in **AFRICA** that are **TRUTHFUL** so that you will not betray yourself.

CONCLUSION B:
AFRICA, THE CENTRE OF THE FIRST SCHOOL GROUND

I know that people do not respect their workshop as they do not respect a school compound and they do not respect teachers. **I AM** going to give a Lecture Revelation about Teachers and what caused their down fall and why teachers are not respected and treated well. **AFRICA** is like a **TEACHER** and it is like **PREACHERS** and there is a reason why people do not treat teachers and preachers very well. The teachers and the preachers are the cause of people not treating them very well because they are those who are supposed to give the **TRUE** picture of a

situation to people. They are supposed
to give the **TRUE** picture of the
ordinance of **GOD**. I give all this Lecture
Revelations to humankind so that they
can be **FREE** from the pending doom
that is coming to the stubborn human
beings on this earth. The first centre of
education and the first playschool
ground is in **AFRICA**. And that is where
Adam learnt about nature and where
the names of everything were given.
That is where I in Adam gave the
names of everything and man started to
take evolution. All natures that were in
spirit started to develop into humankind
to fill everywhere. And I shipped them
away from **AFRICA** to other places to
go and develop. They are all children of
GOD and **GOD** is **THE FATHER** of all
things. And all the things that developed
into human as human animals, human
birds and human fish are all children of
GOD as the servants to **THE FATHER**
GOD and **GOD THE FATHER** however,

that is not what we are talking about today. I have to tell you that people do not respect their workshop. Wherever you create or develop and make things to make millions, you must respect that place and make it beautiful and nice. Sometimes the road that leads that your workshop is very bad but that is where you make serious money to build your mansions to live. Why do you not show respect to the source of your income? Why do you not show respect to the source of your life? This is what has caused many problems for people. **AFRICA** is the **CENTRE** of the **FIRST SCHOOL GROUND** where everything that is learnt comes and that is why from now, the history will be the reverse.

CONCLUSION C:
AFRICA IS ALPHA AND OMEGA, ADAM AND OLUMBA, EVE AND OBU

I have manifested **MYSELF** as **ADAM**. The totality of the **WORD** is **ADAM** as natural but after that, I have been coming in different forms using the same house as the first estate, the senior building of **ADAM**. I have multiplied and photocopied these building a million folds for other human beings therefore; every human being on earth is Adam. **ADAM** means **ALPHA**; the first and all first things are alone. **ADAM** is **ALPHA** and the **OMEGA** as the **SOURCE** and the **DESTINATION** which must link back together. If you cut yourself from the **SOURCE**, then you are finished. If you supply food, the farm where the food comes from is the **SOURCE** even though the food was planted and cultivated by the farmer who is a human being. There are three things in involved in the business of food and they are the farm, the farmer and the trader as the suppliers and the marketers. Who is the supplier? The supplier is the farmer who supplied the food from the farm and sells it to the public for consumption. The question now is that, if you take the food from the farmer in the bad way and you do not pay the farmer well because you think that you have enough, what will you do when it is finished as it surely will? The **SOURCE** is the **FARM** and the **FARMER** as the **SUPPLIER**. And you are the **DESTINATION** where you link the food to the consumers but you must always link back to the **SOURCE** where you get the food from or else when it finishes you and your business will starve. However, the **SOURCE** will always remain as the **SOURCE** which can supply to another **DESTINATION** and say to you 'mister, do not come to me again, I am not distributing my food to you anymore'. For this reason, **AFRICA** being **ADAM**, **ALPHA** as the **FARMER** is the caretaker. And **OLUMBA** is the **DESTINATION** as the

SOURCE of **LIFE** as the **LIFE** itself as **OMEGA** which is also the **DESTINATION** and the **SOURCE** therefore you have to link back. This means that mother **EVE** and mother **OBU** is the same thing. **EVE** is the earth itself and it means **OBU** which is '**NTON**'. Go and ask about the language and it would be explained to you. Evil people turned **OBU** into something else via Satan but this is the **TRUE** talk because **OBU** actually means the dust of the earth and **EVE** means the earth itself. That is **ADAM** and **OLUMBA**, **ALPHA** and **OMEGA** and **EVE** and **OBU** meaning the same thing as the **HEAVEN** and the **EARTH**. A man means the heaven and a woman means the earth. **OLUMBA OLUMBA OBU** means that **THE FATHER** and **THE SON** and the mother **GOD** as the **SPIRIT**, the **SOUL** and the **PHYSICAL**.

That is the end of this part.

Let **MY PEACE** and **BLESSING** abide with the entire world and indeed with **AFRICA**, now and forevermore, *Amien*.

In the name of **OUR LORD JESUS CHRIST**, In the blood of **OUR LORD JESUS CHRIST,** Now ever and forever more, *Amien*.

THANK YOU FATHER

Part Two

AFRICA
THE FOCUS

POINT

In the name of **OUR LORD JESUS CHRIST**, In the blood of **OUR LORD** Jesus **CHRIST** Now ever and forever more, *Amien*.

Today, it pleases **ME THE FATHER GOD OF THE UNIVERSE** to give the second part of the Lecture Revelation titled **THE NIGERIA IN THE AFRICA as AFRICA THE FOCUS POINT**.

INTRODUCTION

As **I** always say, there is no way that anybody can understand the spiritual **WORD** except you tunes yourself to be in spirit. To be in spirit does not mean that you have to initiate yourself in anything. If you want to learn in the English language, you must first learn and understand English. If you want to learn in French you must first learn French. Before you can live with people who speak a different language, you must first learn that language. Every **WORD** is the same in terms of meaning, but the language is not the same. '**DI MI**' and, '**KA KO**' means '**COME HERE**' and '**GO THERE**' in **EFIK** or **IBIBIO**. As you can see, the meaning is the same, but it is matter of language. **I AM THE HOLY SPIRIT**, **THE FATHER GOD** revealing all these things through **MY DIVINE SPIRIT**; therefore, it is up to you to learn the language of the spirit that you will use in understanding the **WORD** of the spirit. And what is that language? **I** will reveal it to you today. The first language is **LOVE**, because if you **LOVE**, you will not reject things outright without knowing anything about that thing. You will not comment badly about anything that you do not know the beginning and the end of. If you **LOVE**, you will always allow **LOVE** to lead you. The second one is to have **UNDERSTANDING**, and **WISDOM**. If you **LOVE**, you will have

PEACE in your spirit and your
PEACEFUL spirit, will open your eye
and that is **WISDOM**. None that has
WISDOM will reject what is **GOOD**, and
they will not allow something that will
lead him or her to lose out for eternity to
control him or her. Another is
ONENESS, and through your heart of
ONENESS, you will have
UNDERSTANDING which is **LOVE**,
and **LOVE** will open a **GOOD** way to
your soul. However, when you see
people that comment wrongly, and
reject things as soon as they hear the
name of a particular person or
something pertaining to something and
say '*oh forget about that*', it means
that they are very, very low in nature.
For this reason, I implore you to have
LOVE, and **HUMILITY**, because those
are the languages that you need in
order to **UNDERSTAND THE
FATHER'S TALK** (**GOD PRESENT**) in
King Solomon Spiritual Library in

general and all the masses of
SUPREME programs that **I** have
brought to change the whole world for
GOOD. The introduction of this Lecture
Revelation is that you must **HUMBLE**
yourself to the **WORD** of **THE FATHER
GOD ALMIGHTY** so that you can
benefit from this recondite open Lecture
Revelations that are not secret. This is
the **SUPREME UNDERSTANDING** and
SUPREME record of **GOD**. This will
enable you to listen with
UNDERSTANDING so that as you have
stood the chance to hear and
UNDERSTAND, you can help others to
also hear and **UNDERSTAND**. From
this basis, the world environment will
become very **GOOD** and blessed for
humankind. What makes **ME THE
FATHER GOD** always destroy the
world? It is because if you do not have
what you want in any product, you will
stop producing that thing. If you cannot
live comfortably in a house, because

water keeps leaking into the house, then you would destroy the house and build another one. However, if your house is **GOOD** and accommodates you, what is the need to destroy it? Instead of that, you stay there and renovate it. What is the need to stop eating the food that is still nice? What is the need to stop planting in the farm that still produces fruit? What is the need to cut down a tree that still bears good fruit? And that is what you must understand. I have no choice than to destroy the whole world if people do not listen to **ME** and think that **GOD** does not exist? It can happen any minute but because of **MY HOLY BLOOD**, and how I was crucified for humankind, **I AM PATIENT**. You must know that the judgement is overdue in this world. Do not forget that all the sins that humans commit and all the abomination that has taken place has made the world so heavy that it can drop down in a second and collapse. The people of this world have sinned so much that it is more than that of Babylon. What is it that people have not done in this world presently, yet **THE FATHER GOD** continues to keep quite? Do you think that you are bribing **ME**? It is because of **MY LONG PATIENCE** so that you will hear and know this **TRUTH**, and be set free by the **TRUTH**. Do you know what brings earthquakes? Earthquakes are the sign of overloaded sin, because I carry the earth in **MY** hand and when the sin of the world is too much, it becomes too heavy to carry. The earth itself moves and is very light, but the sin of the world makes it heavy, and when it becomes too heavy, I turn, and it crakes and that is what causes the earthquake. Any country that sins against **ME** in the nature, the nature visits that country. Sometimes it is in the form of a cyclone, hurricane or a fire disaster and the greatest earthquakes.

It possible that when it becomes too much, it will be total destruction, because when it drops and sinks down and becomes water, then that will be the end of that country. Believe **ME** or not, you must **CHANGE** for **GOOD**. Read the Lecture Revelation titled; **THE GREAT UNIVERSAL CHANGE** and also read and accept the Lecture Revelation titled; **THE SUPREME FUTURE**. Everything that I talk and shout and cry for you is because this is the time of the wilderness, but I will not shout and cry forever. It is only because I want humankind to save their souls. I have so many souls in this world that are **HUMBLE** and consider that **THE FATHER GOD ALMIGHTY** is their **GOD** and everything in life, and as such, they are trying to practice **LOVE**. And that is why I keep quite so that I can give an opportunity for those seeds to germinate and grow, therefore **HUMBLE** your-self and continue to listen to this **WORD** of **THE FATHER GOD**.

A: **AFRICA**, **THE FOCUS POINT**

I have said it in the first part of this Lecture Revelation that you must understand that **AFRICA** is the oldest place on earth, as **THE FATHER** and it is where **MILK** and **HONEY** as the **TREASURE** in a home. I bury every **GOOD** thing in **AFRICA** and that is why upon all that you have stolen from your mother and father's **AFRICA**, it is not finished, because you will still come back to survive there. Today, I want to reveal for you that the spirit soul of King Solomon represents **AFRICA** and western world. When I created King Solomon as incarnate Abel, he was born in Jerusalem. And Jerusalem is a boundary between **AFRICA** and the save side because of the wondering of Abraham. He was looking for where the land was full with **HONEY** and **MILK**.

Honey does not mean physical **HONEY**, it means **PEACE** where **GOD HIMSELF** will rule and everybody will have a life of equality.

What is the story of the prodigal son? It is King Solomon that represents the prodigal son in the Bible. He ate everything of his share of his father's wealth and enjoyed all the glory and power that went with it. He then called it vanity of vanities. Not withstanding all that **GOD** still **LOVED** him, because of his indwelling spirit of **APPRECIATION** to **GOD**. After all that, what happened again? He now has to earmark the posterity of the **WORD** on earth, because he told **ME** to take him as **MY** servant and not as **MY** son. And as a result of that, King Solomon is a servant of **THE FATHER GOD** as he was in the beginning. This is the reason why the western world has taken all the amenities and all the glory and all the post of **WISDOM** that has been established from King Solomon from Ecclesiastes. They have formulated so many things such as science, the power of spiritual ring and so many other things and became very powerful and very rich, but do they worship **THE FATHER GOD**? Since King James edited the Bible and established charity, show **ME** another King or Queen that understands **THE FATHER GOD**. They rather worship elementary spirits and promote dragons and reptiles conducting rituals everywhere. They promote evil; they kill people, go to war and bring woe onto their soul. The only remedy now is for all human races to go back to **AFRICA THE FATHER'S** and **MOTHER'S LAND** as the prodigal son with **LOVE** and **HUMILITY** and learn how to worship **ME THE FATHER GOD THE CREATOR OF THE UNIVERSE** in spirit and in **TRUTH**. This time around, do not go there as you want to rule them or you want to go and steal things from them, because if you do, **I THE FATHER GOD** will be on top of your head. If anybody in this world plans to dupe **AFRICA** even if it is **AFRICANS** themselves, I will wear one leg of trouser and shoe with them. I will wear one leg of trouser with him or her because I will not sit down to see that, that type of thing happens again. I can make your ship or plane to get lost and make anything and even you to become lost if you plan anything against **AFRICA** which is the **FOCUS POINT** as the point of security. I have so many mighty angels in place to the extent that Arch Angel Michael lives in **AFRICA**. And all this is because the wealth of King Solomon is in **AFRICA**, but it is not in the way that you think. This **MY WORD** is the wealth of **THE FATHER GOD** as this Revelation Lecture, because the **FOCUS POINT** of the whole world is in **AFRICA**. The point of

LOVE, the point of **HUMILITY**, the point of **PEACE** and the point of **ONENESS** where there is no segregation, no tribalism and jealousy, strife and arrogance is where **AFRICA** is. Before this period, **AFRICA** was very united. When you meet an **AFRICAN** man naturally, they will give you food and be so hospitable that they can leave their bed for you to sleep in. An **AFRICAN** man can eat the same pot of food with you. A typical **AFRICAN** man is a **POSITIVE GOD THE FATHER'S** representative. When you go to an original **AFRICAN** family who have not copied a light skinned man's ways of an artificial life, the mother, the father and the children all put their hands in the same plate to eat and that is unity. They link from A-Z. All the offspring used to link together until light skin people came and brought so called civilization to separate plates. In the so called civilised world, the mother, the husband, the wife and the children eat from different plates. Light skin people think that eating together is a form of contamination, but people are sleeping together fornicating like dogs in the street, man with man and woman with woman and defect themselves. What contaminates more than fornication and brings more problems into the world than fornication. That is the work of evil. They did that to separate the family of a real **AFRICAN** man so that they betray them. Do you not know that the only people that can betray you are the people that separate you? For instance, why is that when people conduct interviews for an employment position, they do not put everybody in one room and interview them rather they separate them. When they call one person into the room and then call another person into the room, it means that you have something in your heart that you are hiding. That is the meaning of all the meetings that they have. **GOD** speaks in the generality of **LOVE** and **ONENESS** for all, but human beings like to separate things and people.

Do you know when the problem started? It is when the Light Skin man went to **AFRICA** and saw big tress, minerals and many other things that filled the land. They started to think about how they will siphon all these things back to their own land. They saw an old man called the chief of the land as the crowned chief, but the man was very dirty and he did not have any nice clothes. His clothes were tattered and they could not comprehend what he was saying. They established primary free education and brought so called civilization by bringing mirrors, soap, and foreign money to make the people to fall in love with it, but they were all carnal things, as you know that carnal mindedness is death. They were all carnal things as things that did not have any life, and so they brought those things to camouflage **AFRICANS**, just as what Brother Cain gave to **ME** in the past, by offering deadly items as a sacrifice. When they brought all those, things, they picked some people to train and teach them ABC to Z and how to speak their language, because when you speak the language of another person, then you can communicate with them. The Light Skin people or Soft and lighter skin people then selected those that spoke the language instead of those that were supposed to be the chief in the community and through this; they established a Light skin man's government. From there, they called them councillors and administrators and called the natural chiefs traditional rulers. The craftiness of this situation with its long process was all for the purpose of paving the way so that they could steal things from the Solid and

Thick Skin man of **AFRICA**. As part of the process, they bought a staff for the chief of the land that was special decorated painted staff that was nicer than other staffs, and then they bought a cap that was very nice and announced that this person is supposed to be a chief here. After that, they said, how many years have this person been a chief here, yet he cannot speak a foreign language and cannot communicate with us? As a result of the chief not speaking the foreign language, they picked one of the people that they have trained to be a chief and when that happened, the actual spirit of **THE FATHER GOD** left the place and that is when confusion started in the place. That was another way of committing adultery against **ME** the **SUPREME NATURE OF THE WHOLE WORLD IN THE LAND OF AFRICA**. How many countries in **AFRICA** is there rulership through the nature of principle? Do you not know that a person that is to rule is born and cannot be made? Do you not know that if I, **THE FATHER GOD** wants someone to rule a place, I already know the type of spirits that lives there, therefore I will turn **MYSELF** into a human being that would be able to rule everybody to be born there with **WISDOM**. Even if it is a child, I will be in that child to rule. And within that place, everybody would bow to that person, because that person represents **GOD** by nature and he or she would be from a royal family. A royal family always have royal blood as steadiness and a spirit of ruler-ship. However, when you put someone to rule through politics to fight and use books and academia to rule then you frustrate the actual **ROYAL SPIRIT** and that is when you will see woe everywhere with fighting, quarrelling and wars. And that is what is happening in many **AFRICAN** countries. It is because they have driven away the spirit of **ROYAL-HOOD** and replaced it with the spirit of pomposity to rule and that means that it is Satan that is ruling the world and not **GOD**.

I know that some of the politicians, the forceful rulers as the hijackers will not like this Lecture Revelation. Because the positions that they have today, they bought it with money, the wife that they have, they also bought with money because if it is because of handsomeness or character they cannot have such a wife. And this is why everybody is desperate to have money and they would do everything including killing to have money, because money and position makes people to become friends with those who have money. A woman may not like a particular man but because of money, she will marry him. She does not mind kissing the man and later spiting it out because she knows that, that man is not worthy of her love, but because of money she accepts to marry him. Do you not see that you are worshiping demon and Satan? And because of that woe follows you everywhere in the world. Some parts of **AFRICA** are destroyed and spoilt because of woes, cunning, strife and jealousy of people on earth, but it continues to remain the **FOCUS POINT** of the glob. Anything that you do with cunning and arrogance which is not **TRUE** does not belong to you and at the end of the day, you will loose that thing because it is not for you. You must leave things to work naturally. This is why people do not do **GOOD** things again. They do not practice **LOVE** and they do not have a **GOOD** life, because they say to themselves that for all the people that have a **GOOD** life by practicing **GOODNESS** and have **LOVE**, what is actually

GOOD for them? The evil people of this world frustrate them, but I know that they do all these things so that I will become annoyed and destroy them, just as I did in Sodom and Gomorrah and in Babylon. And I have no alternative than to take away that type of spirit, believe **ME** or not this **WORD** shall never fail. It shall come to pass.

AFRICA IS THE FOCUS POINT and every **GOOD** thing goes to **GOOD** things and then stays there for **GOOD** things.

B: **WHY ARE AFRICANS BACKWARD?**

WHY AFRICANS are backward is part of what I have explained in the above chapter. **AFRICANS** are backward because people go to deceive them. For instance, some of the people that go there may say to a woman, 'do you not know that I will make you a queen if you marry me'? 'Look at all the money that I have'. That is the sort of thing that they went and practiced in **AFRICA**. They also said to someone who did not have a single bicycle that they could provide that person with a car and due to this, the person decides to sell his or her land for them but that land is filled with gold. Is this not what happened? You have a child who goes abroad to study and comes back to you as the illiterate parents that gave birth to him but he no longer takes your instruction, because he is now educated. When he arrives, you will say 'my son sit down here' and he will say *'hmm'* as a sigh , 'Daddy, I am not sitting down because I am very busy and I have an appointment in Lagos'. Is that not an insult? When that child was with you, he did not say that to you? A child that thinks that he can speak English will not great you in your dialect again, he will rather great you in

English and that is an insult. You have a friend that has difficulties so you allow him to come and live with you and two of you sleep together on the floor, eat together and generally share the little that you have with him thus the two of you become very tight friends.

However, when this 'friend' becomes lucky and something good happens to come his way, he does not come to see you again. He will say 'oh do not worry, I am very busy now, but I will give you a call sometime, and I am very sorry that I am very, very busy, but I will be in touch'. Now this friend is so busy that he cannot talk to you again and that is what happens in life, but all that is temporal and negative. A **TRUTHFUL** person is what they are and they remain that as they are forever, and that is the principle and the ordinance of someone who is **TRUTHFUL** and represents the **GOOD** part of the **FATHER GOD**. No matter how that person becomes big, if he or she used to talk to you, he or she will still find a way to talk to you. He will still visit you and sit down with you to eat. If you continue to be friendly with the poor people that you used to move with and manage life with before you gained your big man position, will that take your position away? In fact, that position that you have gained is supposed to be for all of you so that you will balance things out a bit and they will benefit from you. The backwardness of **AFRICANS** is caused by lack of **UNDERSTANDING**.

A person that is trained by a dog is indirectly a dog. If a human being gives birth to a child and gives it to a cow to feed, eventually, the child would still look like a human being, but he or she will behave as a cow because it is the energy of a cow that the child has grown up with. The food that you eat forms your physical energy therefore breast milk has the energy of the mother that the milk comes from. A man feeds a woman and the woman feeds the child and that is why children have parents. They are your parents, because they feed you in all capacities including nutrition. If you have a human child, but you use the milk of a cow to feed the child or you give the child to a monkey in the bush to feed eventually, that child will no longer be your child. Even though he or she looks like you, the character will be that of a cow or a monkey. And that is what happens. If you indoctrinate yourself with the evil and negative character in the name of civilisation from **AFRICA** or the western world or any other place which is not from your original template, then you are bringing confusion to your land and yourself. And that means you are destroying yourself and believe **ME**, you are no longer the natural human being that **THE FATHER GOD**, **THE CREATOR** created you to be rather, you become those people. You live with them and copy from them therefore when you come back to your original home; you start to behave like them. Any child that goes to live in America and spends five to seven years there and comes back would start to walk like an American. He will not walk like an **AFRICAN** again. He will not walk with humility. He would walk and jump on the ground and that is exactly what will happen, because of the nature that, that child has acquired which is caused by excessive freedom. **AFRICANS** have a permanent gentlemanly behaviour that is very easy to entreat and merciful. They are all coordinators, as they represent the spoken **WORD**, the first man **ADAM**, because the **TOTAL WORD** lives in **HIM**. They are together in everything. Do not be offended by hearing this from **THE FATHER GOD**, just as I have a Lecture Revelation title; *THE REAL LIGHTER SKIN OR SOFT*

HUMAN (WHITE MAN) IS ANGEL FROM HEAVEN. If you are **TRUTHFUL** and you check for yourself and you see a **TRUTHFUL AFRICAN** in nature, not the artificial one that you call a Black man, the person with black and dark heart, **I** mean the human **GOD**, the **SOLID AFRICAN** human being, you will not like to leave that person. You will be so happy that such a woman or a man is linked with you because he or she would be so nice that he or she will take care of your entire family according to their means. He or she would be so humble and so reasonable and he or she will do anything to make sure that you are happy. Not someone that laughs with you physically, but in their heart their intention is different and they finish you. They would not offend you, but they can finish you off. That is the artificial life that is not from the heart. It is the life of an evolutional human animal, bird or fish. If you are with a man that is a human fish, he may live with you in the house, but in nature, he lives in the water and so you will never in your life be able to corporate with that person. If you live with a woman or man who is a bird in nature, no matter what you do, he or she will always fly away and you will be complaining. If you live with a man or a woman who is an animal, you shall never be close, because anything that he or she does will be done in the bush. All these things are natural, but since you do not know who anyone is, you can only use natural **LOVE** to associate with everybody and maintain your original nature.

The reason that **AFRICANS** are backward in both spirit and soul is because that is where **GOD** lives and that means that Satan also lives there. This is because wherever your front is, that is where your back also is, but what you need to do is to conquer the back and not let your back lead you rather let the front of your self direct you. The same human being has a back and a front, but the back is always backward and the front is always ever forward. You cannot say that **GOD** is in a place and Satan is not there. It is just as wherever, you see **LIGHT** that is where darkness wants to cover but do not forget that **LIGHT** always triumphant against darkness. And if you turn off the **LIGHT** for any reason, the place will be darker than before, but if there was no **LIGHT** to start off with, it would be manageable. This is why **AFRICANS** are backward in so many ways. There are people that are jealous of **AFRICA**, and there are those who think that **AFRICANS** are stupid and they use all types of cunning ways to steal things from them. It is like someone can go to a village and tell the village farmers that, they can buy organic pineapple, coconut, bananas and other fruits from them and say that they will pay them two hundred naira for each basin of a fruit. These village farmers will be so happy but two hundred Naira is about one pound in UK money however when the Lighter skin (White man) takes that to the western world, he would sell that basin for twenty pounds or even more. Despite this, he will still go back to the village farmers and say that the market is not very nice so he would like to pay fifty Naira per basin of fruit so that the market will be nice. And because the village farmers do not have any choice, he will bring them one T. Shirt and a camera that he bought for one pound and when he does that the village farmers will give him the entire farm contents and the land itself and that means that he has bribed the village farmers. And eventually, he would say he would bring a tractor so that the village farmers and him will do the business together and when that happens, he will give the village farmers one farm whilst he takes ten. And that is the type of deception that goes on from people towards innocent **AFRICANS** but everyone that is involved in this way will pay for it because everyman must reap exactly what he or she sows. All of you who have contributed to the backwardness of your father's land will have to go back as the prodigal son and ask for forgiveness and to work as servants for their father. The whole world must say this to their father because, if you have deceived, suppressed and fought against an innocent person, then you must go back and let that person take you back as a servant, without that, there shall be no place on earth for you.

C: **THE FIRST THING IS ALONE**

This is another reason why **AFRICANS** are backwards. It is as though they are very poor and very bad like there is no **GOOD** thing there. Anything that is first is alone. When I, **THE FATHER GOD** established, I was singularly alone. And Adam was also alone. It was only the animals, the birds and fishes that were in place and filled everywhere and that is why it was very easy for them to gang against one man. And it is for this reason that if you're **TRUTHFUL** in the nature of **GOD, THE FATHER** as a real man, you will not have much support because all the animals, fishes and birds will join together and fight against you because the birds of the same feather fly together. What do you think and what are you going to say that is **GOOD**. This is why Satan has established conditions that will favour carnality so that many people will join, but that will only last for a time and then you cause destruction to your soul. You eat what you like and do anything that you want, you kill, you destroy and Satan does not care, because at the end of the day you will destroy your soul with him as an evil spirit. Never forget that anytime that you do something that is not **TRUTHFUL**, and is unfair and negative, you are moving backwards. It means that you are using your back to trade in your life, but it is only the **FRONT** which is the **TRUTH** which **I AM** heading to as the **FORWARDING FUTURE** where all **TRUTHFUL** people will trade with **ME** in the **FRONT** forever.

The **FIRST** thing is always alone. If you bring something **FIRST** and keep it without bringing another, there is no second. If you read the lecture tilted **A-Z**, you will know why Adam was very low in nature. You will also know why the **FIRST** child that is born in a family can behave in a funny way. The **SECOND** child can learn some lessons from the **FIRST**, but the **FIRST** has no predecessor to learn from. Every **FIRST** thing as a **FIRST** wife, **FIRST** children, **FIRST** this and that are always alone and empty, therefore those who always like the first thing have to bear the consequence of being alone as lack of understanding. If you are first in any situation, know that you lack some level of **UNDERSTANDING**. If you talk **FIRST** in a meeting know that you **LACK EXPERIENCE** of the issues that others may have. If you are the **FIRST** to be appointed to anything, you have to put yourself in prayer because people will take what you say to correct their mistakes. The **FIRST** thing is always empty and alone and that is what has brought the downfall of **AFRICA** and the Dark Thick Skinned man. However, the **HISTORY** is now **CHANGED**.

D: THE DOWNFALL OF AFRICA IS SIN

If you have no experience and knowledge then you end up misunderstanding things and that is sin. Anything that you do wrongly is sin and that is the power of Satan and evil. All the dirty and evil things that people do as not talking well, and not reasoning well are because of the negativism that is part and parcel of all raw materials. Any raw material that has not been divined is a bad thing. Some foods are poisonous but if you take away the negative part which is the poison, it becomes an edible product. Anything that is raw may not be perfect. Even I **THE FATHER GOD** was not **DIVINABLE PHENOMENON** until I **DIVINED MYSELF** as the **HOLY SPIRIT OF TRUTH**. However when you attach yourself to the part that is **NOT DIVINED** called the **WHOLE** then that is where you sacrifice and do all sorts of bad things and excuse yourself that it is from **GOD THE FATHER**. Yes, everything is **GOD THE FATHER** but you must act on the **POSITIVE SIDE OF THE FATHER GOD** which is the **DIVINED** part, called the **HOLY SPIRIT OF TRUTH**. **THE FATHER GOD** is **ALL** and **ALL** but **ALL** and **ALL** are no longer accepted back to **THE FATHER GOD**, because I have **DIVINED MYSELF**. And this is why sin is the downfall of **AFRICAN** nations and they have pass it to the entire world, because the **AFRICAN** man was created as the image and likeness of **GOD** and that is why if an **AFRICAN** man sins it affects them more that when any other type if person sins. And that is why the blood that the **AFRICAN** man has is more powerful than any other type of blood in this world, because it is only a solid and thick liquid that can change anything in this world to be more colourful. Today, I have brought this knowledge and understanding to all **AFRICAN** humans or those of you that call yourself a black man, but you should know that no human being is black or white, all humankind are either thick and solid with a strong skin or soft and light with a weak skin. What I want is for you to stop practicing evil. You should stop doing things that are counterfeit and not from your original self. Stop fighting against one another. And any position that you have whether it is political or natural, must be exercised with the natural **LOVE** of **ONENESS** for the whole world. You must use it to unite with everyone, because the whole world is **ONE**, originating from **THE FATHER GOD'S LAND** which is **AFRICA**. And without **AFRICA**, the world will not be civilised and developed and also without the thick skinned man serving the whole world, the world would not progress because a father must first serve his children. If you go anywhere in the world, you will find that the Thick Skin people are servants because they are servants of the **LORD** as your father and your mother. That is why if you are called a servant, do not be offended because it only **GOD** that serves. The Thick Skin man represents the **SPOKEN WORD**. And it is the **WORD** that serves everybody therefore; do not be ashamed to be in the position of servitude because apart from **THE FATHER GOD**, the next person is the **SERVANT** of **GOD**, which is the **SPOKEN WORD**, the **LOVER** of **GOD**. These are those who **LOVE GOOD** things and want things to be **GOOD** forever.

E: **THE FIRST SHALL BE THE LAST**

The problem that Esau had was that he was a servant, as such he did everything to help his old father, but the mother cognized with Jacob and took his blessing and gave it to Jacob but at the end of the day, **THE FIRST THAT HAS BECOME THE LAST BUT YOU WILL SEE WHAT WILL HAPPEN AT THE LAST**. The first shall become the last because of being humble and alone as a servant and not having any experience. The first was created alone and remained stupid; not being beautiful because of too much work as such could not do anything. Being in that position means that sometimes, you cook for people but you do not eat. And sometimes despite all that you do people do not recognize you but do not worry because you shall reap all that you sow and that is a **WORD** that is enough for the wise.

F: **HE WHO LAUGHS AT THE LAST HAS THE BEST LAUGHTER**

The point now is that **WHO EVER THAT LAUGHS LAST, LAUGHS THE**

BEST but who is that person that laughs the last? It is the person that people reject and forget about and sometimes, they cognize against. It is usually someone that does **GOOD** and because of that people do not like to involve him or her in what they do because if they do so, he or she spoils their plans. There are some people that when you mention their name, people think that upon their arrival within a place, they will not accept the negative plans because they are straight forward and **TRUTHFUL** and because of that they do not put such people in their gangs. Such people do care because they are directed by the spirit of **TRUTH**. If someone is **TRUTHFUL** in the government, they will not like to vote for him. When they go and have their meetings, they will say, 'do not involve this person in such and such because we will not be able to steal any money if he or she is here'. However this is **THE TIME FOR THOSE WHO LAUGH THE LAST TO LAUGH THE BEST**. From the year OH (eight) of this century, it is only **TRUTHFUL** people that will be in the government and only the **TRUTHFUL** people that will be in charge in the family. It is the **TRUTHFUL** people that will marry other **TRUTHFUL** people and it is only the **TRUTHFUL** souls that would be born into the family and it is only the **TRUTHFUL** people that would hold all positions in the government and in all organizations because the **SPIRIT OF TRUTH** has come to manage the world by itself and the **TRUTH** shall set us **FREE**. And this is why those who **LAUGH THE LAST LAUGH THE BEST** because you shall now reap the fruit of your labour as the **FIRST**.

G: **AFRICA IS THE FATHER GOD**

AFRICA IS THE FATHER GOD means the **SPIRIT**. All the minerals and

the resources that I bless are in
AFRICA. It is not only **AFRICA** that I
have blessed, but the blessing of the
father who will share for his children is
more than other blessings. There are so
many things all over the world but you
will realise that I have **TRANSCENDED**
the soul of **POSITIVISM** and **GOOD**
things back to **AFRICA** to help them to
LAUGH THE LAST and that is why the
hope of the whole world is dependent
on I, **THE FATHER GOD THE
CREATOR OF THE UNIVERSE** and
AFRICA represents **THE FATHER
GOD** as the **FIRST** which is also the
last and that is **ALPHA** and **OMEGA**.
The **CYCLE RING** means the **SOURCE**
and the **DESTINATION** therefore you
must get into that ring before you can
survive because that is where I
preserve **LIFE** and **SOUL** and that is
also where I preserve the **GLORY** of
GOD on earth.

CONCLUSION A:
AFRICA, THE SOURCE AND THE DESTINATION

AFRICA IS THE SOURCE AND THE DESTINATION. The **SOURCE** is **LOVE, PEACE, HARMONY, ONENESS, HUMILITY, MERCY, PATIENCE** and **THE DESTINATION** is the **TRUTH**. And that is why all the **GOOD** virtues are managed by the **TRUTH** because if you are not **TRUTHFUL** all these things are rubbish. You can have **LOVE** but without being **TRUTHFUL LOVE** does not mean anything. Equally, you can have **MERCY** but because it is not **TRUTHFUL** it may only last for the morning but by evening, it is gone. Anything that you do without **TRUTH** has no meaning and that is why the **DESTINATION OF THE FATHER GOD** is **TRUTH** and the **SOURCE** is that **GOD** is **EVERYTHING**. The **TRUTH** as the **DESTINATION** is where everybody needs to go and that will link you back to **THE FATHER GOD** who is **EVERYTHING**.

CONCLUSION B:
AFRICA IS THE MAKER OF MAKERS

As **AFRICA** is the **SOURCE** and **DESTINATION**, it is the **MAKER OF MAKERS**. **AFRICA** means the **BEGINNING** as **ADAM** and **EVE**. Scientist and everybody know this. It is not a means of pride, but **AFRICA** means the whole world and **AFRICA** means the blessing of **THE FATHER GOD** for everybody, therefore, find your way in **PEACE** to **AFRICA**, your home where **RIGHTEOUSNESS**, **PEACE** and **JOY** exist and shun all misbehaving. Stealing, evil spirits and everything must join the **NEW DISPENSATION** of **POSITIVE, POSITIVE** and **POSITIVE SPIRIT** of **GOOD** behaviours that will establish in **AFRICA**. Every country in **AFRICA** is the kingdom of **GOD** and **I, THE FATHER GOD** will reveal **MYSELF** there in a big way. And the whole world shall see! If you go on holiday in **AFRICA** you will be happy because **AFRICA** likes everybody especially strangers because that is your home. **AFRICA** is **GOD** therefore; I will destroy all the witch and wizards that operate in **AFRICA**. When you have **LOVE**, I will use that to save you and that is why I have sent millions of **POSITIVE** angels to **AFRICA** so that all you will hear of is **FATHER GOD**, **FATHER GOD** and **FATHER GOD**. People say that even though it is **GOD**, **GOD**, **GOD** there is too much evil. Yes there is, but not a lot of evil, however, the evil that is present now, is temporal because the seed of **THE FATHER GOD** has already germinated there therefore give **ME** some time and you will see what **AFRICA** will become.

AFRICA is the **LEADER** and **MAINTAINER OF THE WHOLE UNIVERSE**.

CONCLUSION C:
YOU MUST LOVE TO UNDERSTAND THIS WORD

It is only if you **LOVE** and have the **HOLY SPIRIT** and **WISDOM** that you will treasure this **FATHER'S TALK (GOD PRESENT)** as the **WORD** of **EVERLASTING RECORD** from the **SUPREME MEMORY OF GOD**. It is only when you have **LOVE** that you will not ask who said this **WORD** and where the mouth is that spoke this **WORD** and who witnessed it is? Do you worry about the box of television as to whether it is big or small? All that you know is that you have seen the picture and heard the sound and also seen the programme. That is how you acknowledge what is **GOOD**. It is only those who have **LOVE** and are

POSITIVE that will take this **WORD** and blessed are they and their soul because when you accept this **TRUTH** then you are **FREE**, now and forever, more, *Amien*.

Let **MY PEACE** and **BLESSING ABIDE** with the entire world, now and forever, more, *Amein*.

In the name of **OUR LORD JESUS CHRIST**,
In the blood of **OUR LORD** Jesus **CHRIST**
Now and forever more, *Amien*.

THANK YOU FATHER

Part Three

In the name of **OUR LORD JESUS CHRIST**, In the blood of **OUR LORD** Jesus **CHRIST** Now ever and forever more, *Amien*.

THE NIGERIA IN THE AFRICA

LEADER OLUMBA OLUMBA OBU, THE FINAL WORD IN PERSON, THE NIGERIA, THE CENTRE OF EXCELLENCE AND INTELLECT, THE HOME OF GOD, THE HOME OF PEACE AND THE HOME OF THE SUPREME WORD MANIFESTATION

Today, it pleases **ME THE FATHER GOD, THE CREATOR OF THE UNIVERSE, THE SUPREME WORD** that manifest everything to give the part three of this Lecture Revelation, **THE**

NIGERIA IN THE AFRICA titled **OLUMBA OLUMBA OBU, THE FINAL WORD IN PERSON, THE NIGERIA, THE CENTRE OF EXCELLENCE AND INTELLECT, THE HOME OF GOD, THE HOME OF PEACE AND THE HOME OF THE SUPREME WORD MANIFESTATION.**

INTRODUCTION:

NIGERIA IS A PLACE IN THE CORNER OF THE WORLD THAT IS THE BIRTH PLACE OF THE HOLY SPIRIT OF TRUTH PERSONIFIED

NIGERIA is the **CENTRE** as the **MANAGER** where the **WORD** came to be in fruition and it is where the final **WORD** personified physically. **I THE FATHER GOD** planed this and that is the meaning of one who laughs last, laughs the best. I know that so many negative satanic people in the world have made many things. They have gone to the sea and brought mud and gone to many places to bring charcoal to cover **NIGERIA**, because they have heard that **LEADER OLUMBA OLUMBA OBU** came from and was born in **NIGERIA**. People have done so many things and said many things such as **OLUMBA** drinks blood, **OLUMBA** is Satan, **OLUMBA** is juju and **OLUMBA** is this and that but all that is to take the mind of people away from the **LIGHT** that has manifested in the **WORLD**.

Is it **TRUE** that **OLUMBA** drinks blood? Is it **TRUE** that **NIGERIA** in **AFRICA** is the worse place? Is it **TRUE** that you cannot find anything **GOOD** in **NIGERIA**? This is what people say? Some years ago, in spirit, the entire world had a meeting in the synagogue of Satan and agreed that they would bring the synagogue of Satan to **NIGERIA**. The synagogue of Satan was originally established in Egypt and they moved it to Babylon then from Babylon, they moved it to California and from there, they moved it to **AFRICA** and wanted to bring it to **NIGERIA** but I said **NO-WAY**, because there cannot be two seats in one place! Since, **I THE FATHER GOD** has established the seat of the **HOLY SPIRIT**; no other seat can survive in **NIGERIA**. If you observed, some years ago so many people were born in Nigeria that were evil so that they would cause misunderstanding and practice all amounts of havoc. There were criminals upon criminals as the worst criminals on earth born in **NIGERIA**. And for that I sent trips of the best human being as the most **INTELLIGENT**, and the most **EXCELLENT** spirits as *Arch angel Michael, Holy Spirit Gabriel*, I also sent King Solomon, because I **THE SUPREME WORD** manifested in **NIGERIA**, as the **HOLY SPRIT OF TRUTH**. The **KING OF KINGS** and the

LORD OF LORD, in addition many **POSITIVE** human souls to be born in **NIGERIA** so that we will see what will happen. I meant it, that is exactly what I did and I **AM** speaking about it today. I, **MYSELF** physically manifested there, because If **NIGERIA** or **AFRICA** spoils like any other place in the world then it means that the seat of **GOD** is polluted with evil and for that reason, I put **MY** feet down. They even tried to bring the head quarter of witchcraft from India and put it in **NIGERIA**.

If you go anywhere, you will find that they have chosen many **NIGERIAN** men to be the head of any juju, witchcraft and other satanic and evil practices, because wherever the **LIGHT** is, that is where darkness wants to go. And because they cannot succeed, they say that **OLUMBA OLUMBA OBU** is Satan and evil. Show **ME** where you see **OLUMBA** being Satan? Read all the **WORD** from **OLUMBA** who is the final personified **WORD** that manifested on earth as the **HOLY SPIRIT PERSONIFIED**. The **FATHER** has come in Adam, the son, the **WORD** and as **JESUS THE CHRIST** and **OLUMABA**, **OLUMBA OBU** came as **THE HOLY SPIRIT** of **TRUTH**. And if you know this spirit of **TRUTH**, you are **FREE** forever. This **HOLY SPIRIT OF TRUTH** was born in **NIGERIA**, as the spiritual centre of **THE GLOBATAL 'THECOMITAN' in AFRICA** so now what do you want to tell **ME**. I do not speak so that you will like it; **I** speak to keep the testimony for eternity. Some people open their eyes here on earth by taking correction on this present plane and others take correction in prison and some people open their eyes when they die in hell, because evil people only take correction in hell. It is **GOOD** to take correction in the **TRUTH**, so that it is not too late for you to amend things, but if you wait until you die then it becomes too late. If you wait until you take correction in hell, it is too late and if you wait until you take correction in prison, it is equally too late, and therefore it is up to you to make your choice.

The introduction of this Lecture Revelation is the **NIGERIA THE CENTRE OF EXCELLENCE AND INTELLECTUALS**, the **HOME OF GOD** because **I THE FATHER GOD**, the **SPOKEN WORD, LEADER OLUMBA OLUMBA OBU** has manifested here in person. **I AM** the **PERSONIFIED HOLY SPIRIT OF TRUTH** as the **DIVINE PART OF THE FATHER GOD** that has finally taken an assumed body to put things right in the world. And you will see **ME *EVERYWHERE*, *HERE*** and ***THERE*** and I become everything of everything positive for all men and women. Wherever you are in your cycle, in your meeting, and in your position, **I AM** the chairperson there. And whenever you plan and it is negative, at the end of the day, I thwart it. Who do you think thwarts the entire evil plan in the world? It is the spirit of **THE FATHER GOD**. This is because you cannot do anything without the **WORD**, therefore by **THINKING, I AM** the **ONE**, by **SPEAKING, I AM** the **ONE** and by **HEARING, I AM** the **ONE** by writing or **DOING THE ACTION, I AM** the **ONE**, therefore which **ONE** are you among the four? **I AM** the **ENERGY** and the **ACTIVATOR** of life because **I AM EVERYTHING** of **EVERYTHING**, therefore **I AM** the only **ADAUSUNG** and **I AM LEADING EVERYWHERE, HERE** and **THERE** even if you do not believe anything it does not mean anything to **ME**. Even when you do not **BELIEVE** this **WORD**, it is **THE FATHER GOD** and when you **BELIEVE**, it is equally **THE FATHER**

GOD. WHATSOEVER, WHATSOEVER, it is **THE FATHER GOD WHATSOEVER**; therefore, I have no problem in **WHATSOEVER**.

A: **NIGERIA IS WHERE RIVER NIGER IS IN THE MIDDLE OF THE CITY EARTH**

There is a lot of mystery and a lot of things that happen in **NIGERIA** and one day I will tell the whole world why I created **RIVER NIGER** there. The **RIVER NIGER** is called the **CRYSTAL IN THE MIDDLE OF GOD'S CITY**. The **RIVER NIGER** is a special river in the whole world and that is why it passes through the middle of the city in **NIGERIA** in between the north, south, west and the east. It is **THE FATHER GOD** that best knows why the **RIVER** is where it is and it is what attracted **MY** nature to reside there as the **HOLY SPIRIT**. And from there all principalities bow down.

B: **THE UNIVERSAL SUPREME MYSTERY IS THE COUNTRY OF NIGERIA**

The country **NIGERIA in AFRICA** is the **UNIVERSAL SUPREME MYSTERY** country and no human being on this earth can tell you what is in **NIGERIA** and the meaning of **NIGERIA** because no one knows. It is a situation of the more you look, the less you see and the more you hear, the less you understand, but leave **NIGERIA** for **THE FATHER GOD** and leave their condition and way of Life to **THE FATHER GOD** because the living shall see what is going to happen in **NIGERIA**. However, **I AM** telling you that there is a **MYSTERY** that is beyond the human way in **NIGERIA,** therefore, uses **HUMILITY**, **LOVE** and **PEACE** to treat all **NIGERIANS** and if you see any **NIGERIAN** anywhere, treat the person with honour. However, if you see any

NIGERIAN man or woman that behaves with arrogance and pomposity and is negative, then he or she is not a **TRUE NIGERIAN** by nature, because they have missed their way by being born there and eventually they will not be born there again. I have fenced around **NIGERIA** and all **AFRICAN COUNTRIES AND IN DEED THE WHOLE WORLD**, and eventually, I will send angels to clean all places and send all rubbish away and you will see that every place will be very nice. In the **WORD** of **GOD**, I have said that the owner of the farm plants his **GOOD** seed in the day time, but in the night, the evil one goes and plants a counterfeit seed so that when they germinate, the farmer would be confused. However when the plants start to bear fruit, clarity will arise, because 'by their fruit ye shall know them'. **In NIGERIA, THE FATHER'S LAND**, you will **LOVE** to see the children of **GOD** that are there with **WISDOM, UNDERSTANDING, HUMILITY, FASTNESS** in **UNDERSTANDING, CLEVERNESS, INTELLECT** and all **GOOD** and **POSITIVE** virtues. However when you see thief's, arm robbers, dupers and evil people and all sorts of bad people, then know that those are the bad seeds that Satan has planted there to use them to spoil **NIGERIA** in the **AFRICA**. As it is presently, people would say that there is no guarantee deal delivery to **NIGERIA** and there is no guarantee this and that in **NIGERIA** and that is the work of evil so that people will be afraid to do any business with **NIGERIANS**.

When evil wants to spoil your family, it will make your children to become stubborn and make your wife to become disobedient. When everybody around you becomes difficult, it is because they want to spoil your record, but **THE FATHER GOD** has now corrected that, because **I** have taken over. Do you know why your children become stubborn and your wife becomes untrustworthy, and everybody around you becomes difficult? It is because enemies know that you are with the **LIGHT**, and they use them to destroy you so that no one will write home about you? Since **THE FATHER GOD** has lifted up his hands to band all principalities around you then it is banned and everything changes for **GOOD**. And that is why **NIGERIA** is the **SUPREME MYSTERY COUNTRY** on earth.

C: **THE NIGERIA IS IN AFRICA, THE FATHER GOD'S PLACE OF BIRTH**

In the beginning **I THE FATHER GOD** broke the egg of life there and at the end; **I THE FATHER GOD** manifested the **HOLY SPIRIT OF TRUTH** as the final **SUPREME WORD**

PERSONIFIED. And now in **AFRICA** you will find the final reincarnated Adam as the **UNIVERSAL SHRINE** in **NIGERIA**. Check it well in your spiritual self if you are a spirited or have where you go to check things then tell this **WORD** to that spiritual self and if it is a **TRUTHFUL** spiritual self, it will tell you that the reincarnated Adam is in **NIGERIA** as the **KING** of **KINGS** and the **LORD** of **LORDS**. And that is where the whole world will pay homage and those who do that shall be blessed.

D: **NIGERIA IS WHERE ABEL SHOWED HIS FIRST APPRECIATION TO GOD**

After I sent Adam and Eve from the Garden of Eden, I pushed the children across the **RIVER NIGER** which was a little lake at the time, but it is now a big river that ends in the Atlantic Ocean from the south, north, east and west **(EAWENOSO ENERGY OF GOD)**.

This is where Abel **APPRECIATED GOD**, (not sacrificed) and that is where Cain killed Abel. And due to that blood there, I earmarked the place. Somewhere in **NIGERIA** called **YEBU ODE** kingdom is where Queen Sheba's palace was built to represent where Abel was killed and that is why from today, I have blessed **NIGERIA** and taken away spirit of negativism and returned their son back to them as HRM King Solomon David Jesse **ETE**. He was taken away because when people hate you in a place, I take you away from there just as when they hated **CHRIST** his Father in Jerusalem, I took him to Egypt where I will tell you what is happening there now. **ETHIOPIA** shall arise! And that is why **NIGERIA** is a **MYSTERIOUS** country and it is filled with a lot of positive secrets, but it is only **THE FATHER GOD** that knows the secret of his kingdom.

E: HALLE-SELASSIEI WAS ANOTHER TRANSIT OF ABEL WHICH IS THE SAME KING SOLOMON.

I was **HALLE-SELASSIEI** in Abel to go and help **AFRICA** to establish the link of prayer to represent the land where Abel was killed. This was so that when he prayed, and prayed and prayed and prayed and worried, **GOD** listened to him and returned the blessing back to **AFRICA. HALLE-SELASSIEI** was the original rebirth spirit of Esau which was ABEL, the lion of **AFRICA** but I have now changed him back to his original self as King Solomon, the spiritual man for his people.

F: ETHIOPIA SHALL ARISE

Now **ETHIOPIA** has arisen by **GOD HIMSELF** because it only **THE**

FATHER GOD that can bless his child. When the family falls because of a bad child, the family can only be reconstituted when the father reincarnates back into the family. And that is what always happens. If a family spoils because of a child, then when the father is reborn in that family, he will refurbish the family because it is only the father that replaces things. It is **I THE FATHER GOD THE CREATOR OF THE UNIVERSE** that created **AFRICA** and now, the whole world has to return back to **MY** home base where I will replace all evil with **GOOD** spirits and then everything will be well there. All demons, all water spirits souls, all incantations, all secret societies, all witchcraft, all idles and all negativisms that operate in **AFRICAN COUNTRIES** because of lack of **UNDERSTANDING** will all turn to the **HOLY SPIRIT** and worship the **HOLY SPIRIT OF TRUTH**. It will be joy, joy and joy that will reign in

AFRICA and the whole world shall see the glory of **GOD** manifest there. And that is where HRM king Solomon **ETE** will build the final **UNIVERSAL SUPREME MERCY SHRINE** for **THE SUPREME WORD** for eternity.

G: THE NIGERIA IN THE AFRICA WELCOMES THE HOLY SPIRIT OF TRUTH PERSONIFIED

Since **NIGERIANS** believe that the **HOLY SPIRIT OF TRUTH** is in **NIGERIA** to inspire and possess, just as **HRM King SOLOMON ETE** is possessed by the **HOLY SPIRIT OF TRUTH** "*GOD'S DIVINE WISDOM*" then, I pour the **HOLY SPIRIT** onto **NIGERIA** and other **AFRICAN COUNTRIES** that believe. This is why people wonder why everywhere in this world, there are **NIGERIANS** doing one thing or the other. The most powerful preachers, teachers, and workers of many fields of works anywhere in

NIGERIA, **AFRICA** and the whole World are **NIGERIANS**, and it has even not started yet! This is another promotion for **NIGERIA**, **NIGERIA** and **NIGERIA**! And HRM King Solomon David Jesse **ETE** is a **NIGERIAN**. And people wonder why he should have the same name. Let **ME** tell you how it managed. His grandfather became Jesse through some missionaries that went to visit **NIGERIA**. There was one particular missionary that **I** sent by manipulation in the transit in the time of Mary Slessor who was in Calabar, Akwa-Ibom State in Itu. These missionaries went to ministry work in Ikot Abasi in Opobo division to establish a church. It happened that there was no church in the place at the time. At that time it was Ekpo Masquerade that used to be the traditional worship that everybody worshiped. When the missionaries established a church, Ekpo Masquerade said that they will never establish a church, but the granddad of King Solomon accepted the innovation, because I sent him there for that purpose as the original Jesse to establish the womb again in that part of the world. This is the world without end, and it means the **WORD** without end. It is because of him that I sent those missionaries there, and once they baptised him, they gave him a baptismal name as Jesse. Nobody told them anything and his name prior to that was Akpan Udoh Utin-Idem Akapn esien Ibanga Okwo which means 'the self sun'. Utin is the sun and idem means self, but because they could not understand the name, they gave him Jesse and Jesse in the original Hebrew means the tribe as the offspring and that is where David came from. And then they gave Jesse the Holy Bible named him Elder Jesse and the father that established the community where Jesse came from was called **ETE** which means an older person or the Father of the Land and he was the King, who owned that land. And according to tradition the first son should be named after their grandfather so when Jesse had his first son, he called him David, now when David had his first son he name him Jesse is father and named his the second son Solomon- hence we now have Solomon David Jesse **ETE**, and tell **ME** whether it is an accident. And this is Solomon David Jesse **ETE** that **I AM** talking through now and his biography that **I AM** giving you through this **AFRICA-HOOD**, because nobody can hide the will of **GOD**. **I AM** giving you this story by **MYSELF**, but you can say that it is King Solomon or you can say anything that you like. You can also go and talk your own, but the **TRUTH** shall set you **FREE**. **I AM** the **SPIRIT** that **POSSESS** HRM King Solomon **ETE** in the original spiritual way that has brought him back on earth. And

HUMILITY is his way of life and **PEACE** is his insurance and **TRUTH** as his **ROYAL-HOOD**, therefore his HRM King Solomon **ETE** is **MY** talking and talking **SELF**.

NIGERIANS have welcomed the **HOLY SPIRIT PERSONIFIED** and they are blessed for it. And since they have welcomed **THE FATHER GOD**, there is no segregation anymore and if you go to **NIGERIA**, it is about **THE FATHER GOD** and **THE FATHER GOD** and everywhere in the whole world is about **THE FATHER GOD** and **THE FATHER GOD**. It is only small evil people that pretend that they do not know **THE FATHER GOD**, but everyone in **NIGERIA** knows **THE FATHER GOD**. Everybody in **NIGERIA** knows **LEADER OLUMBA**. Previously they used say **OLUMBA** did this and **OLUMBA** did that, but now nobody says those things again because they know the **TRUTH**.

If you go in the fold of Brotherhood you will find that some are witches and wizards, but they are there pretending to be **TRUE** Brotherhood members. If you go to any church, you will find both **GOOD** and bad people whether in Light skin or Thick skin people, but that does not mean that the particular place is **GOOD** or bad, because **THE FATHER GOD** is in-charge of the whole world. However, what will happen now is that **GOD** stands for **TRUTH** therefore all **TRUTH** shall remain and bad shall be eliminated. And since the **NIGERIA** is the birth place of the **HOLY SPIRIT PERSONIFIED** and the centre of operation, **THE FATHER GOD** has blessed them and that has attracted all **POSITIVE SELVES** of **GOD** to manifest in **NIGERIA**. And **I** have now assigned and multiplied GB (seventy two) million **POSITIVE** selves of King Solomon to be born everywhere in the world and **NIGERIA** to be the servants of **GOD** and a lot of them have already been born.

CONCLUSION A:
OLUMBA OLUMBA OBU, THE FINAL WORD IN PERSON, THE FINAL PHYSICAL HOUSE OF THE SUPREME WORD

I do not live in the house that man builds. And **I** created Adam and lived in Adam to manage the whole world, as the **KING** of **KINGS** and **LORD** of **LORDS** and the only **LEADER (ADAUSUNG) THE SPIRITUAL ADMINISTRATOR**. When you talk about the **KING of KINGS** and the **LORD OF LORDS**, it is the **SUPREME WORD**. And when you talk about man, it is where the **WORD** lives, therefore every **POSITIVE** human being that represents the real **GOD** is a King and their **FATHER** is the **KING OF KINGS** and the **LORD OF LORDS**. **OUR LORD JESUS CHRIST** was the **KING**

OF KINGS, because he was incarnate Adam, therefore as daughters and sons of **GOD** you are **KINGS QUEENS** and **PRINCES** and **PRINCESSES because** your father Adam is the **KING OF KINGS** and the **LORD OF LORDS**. And now the new Adam has arrived as the **PERSONIFIED HOLY WORD** without end as the divine house and **SHRINE** and that is posterity for humankind for eternity. And all human beings that accept this are blessed and if you do not accept, then it means that you have disgraced yourself.

CONCLUSION B:
IT IS ONLY EVIL THAT HATES WHAT IS GOOD AND ONLY SATAN THAT DENIES THE TRUTH

What is evil and what is Satan? I have now divined it. Evil is a mistake and lack of understanding. It is primitive, lacking **WISDOM** and anything that is low and negative as evil and a counterfeit thing. It is only evil and bad things that mean Satan, because Lucifer could not accept, acknowledge and worship **THE UNIVERSAL SUPREME WORD** and accept that man to be in charge to represent the house of all spiritual soul, which is the mistake that Lucifer has made for eternity and cannot forgive **ITSELF**. That is the greatest mistake that any man can make and if you also make the same mistake by asking how man can be **GOD** then you are also negative. You are speaking aren't you? You are not **GOD**, but you are able to bring another human being into this world. And the **LIGHT** of the world is the **SPOKEN WORD** and that is **GOD,** but it is not **THE ALMIGHTY THE FATHER GOD**, and that is why you are representing **THE FATHER GOD** and at the same time representing **GOD THE SUPREME WORD** as the son of **GOD**, and at the same time you are also **GOD** yourself. It is only when you are evil that you will misunderstand this **WORD**, because you are ABC quasi-quack, because the **HOLY SPIRIT** is not in you and you are alone. And that is what happened to Adam when he was alone, and is what will happen to you. And if you're alone, you will say that this **WORD** is not from **THE FATHER GOD** rather it is a human being talking, and you will misinterpret this **WORD**, because you also misinterpret your life. And for that, I do not blame you, because you are a miniature human being as a human bird, human animal and human fish. However, if you are a real human **GOD** with understanding and a **TRUTHFUL SPIRIT** you will understand that this **WORD** is from **THE FATHER GOD**. And it is **GOOD** to **BELIEVE** and **ACCEPT** and join HRM King Solomon to celebrate the **UNIVERSAL SUPREME WORD SEASON**

CELEBRATION that is **GOD** now on earth.

CONCLUSION C:
THE TRUTH IS AN UNCHANGEABLE PHENOMENON

The **TRUTH** is an **UNCHANGEABLE PHENOMENON** because since the **TRUTH** has been declared, that stands forever as you cannot change the **TRUTH**. Check it well and you will realise that people do not like the **TRUTH**, because they represent lies, evil, Satan and negativism. Those who resent **GOD**, **GOOD** and **POSITIVISM** like the **TRUTH**, because the **TRUTH** does not need too much interpretation just as this Lecture Revelation does not require interpretation. If you like the **TRUTH**, take it and if you do not like it then leave it, but in your heart, you will know that it is **TRUE**, because your conscience will tell you that it is **TRUE**. However, if you make the mistake of

saying that this **WORD** is not the
TRUTH, then you are not going to be
maintained by the positive **SUPREME**
WORD in you, and that is hell because
your soul will be rebuked and reduced
to nothing since you refuse to accept
the **TRUTH** you will not have a sound
mind any longer. People go about and
speak evil about Brotherhood of the
Cross and Star, because some evil
people have joined Brotherhood to
destroy it and they are the evil agents.
Some evil people do a lot of things,
because they say that Brotherhood is
the **LIGHT** so they come to quench the
LIGHT, but you can never quench the
LIGHT. I know many people that are in
Brotherhood including preachers that
are evil messengers. Indeed all things
are Brotherhood including Satan,
therefore why do you doubt if you see
Satan in Brotherhood and if you see
bad people doing bad things in
Brotherhood. You should know however

that Brotherhood is divided into two capacities as negative and **POSITIVE**. The **POSITIVE** part is the **HOLY SPIRIT OF TRUTH** which is directed by the **DIVINE SELF, LEADER OOOBU**. And the negative part is the old Brotherhood directed by the Vampire the soul of Cain the first son of Adam, and it is for those who practice evil and do all sorts of negative practices incantations and all over the world. If you say that you are not Brotherhood, you are a typical liar, because Brotherhood means everything created by **THE FATHER GOD** and even Satan knows this. And that is why the truth is **AN UNCHANGEABLE PHENOMENON WHICH IS THE SAVIOUR OF HUMANKIND AND THE POSITIVE SPIRIT OF THE FATHER GOD**.

Let **MY PEACE** and **BLESSING** abide with all of humankind and all

NIGERIANS, **AFRICANS** and the entirety of **THE UNIVERSE** and indeed all citizens of the world now and forevermore.

In the name of **OUR LORD JESUS CHRIST**
In the blood of **OUR LORD** Jesus **CHRIST**
Now and forever more *Amien*.

THANK YOU FATHER

PART FOUR

THE INSPIRATIONAL WRITER

-

KING SOLOMON SPIRITUAL LIBRARY
THE GOD ENCYCLOPAEDIA WORD OF INFINITY

INSPIRATIONAL WRITERS AND READERS OF THE FATHER'S TALK
(GOD PRESENT)
KING SOLOMON SPIRITUAL LIBRARY

In the name of our Lord Jesus Christ In the blood of our Lord Jesus Christ Now and forever more, Amen

(A) REFERENCING THE FATHER'S TALK (GOD PRESENT) IN KING SOLOMON SPIRITUAL LIBRARY

I know some people will inspire when you visit King Solomon Spiritual Library website or bookshop, and have access to any of **THE FATHER'S TALK (GOD PRESENT)** information through books, electronics, audio and otherwise and are inspired to write or produce any information through the knowledge that you have gained, you must not fail to reference **THE FATHER'S TALK (GOD PRESENT)** in **King Solomon Spiritual Library** as the such of your inspirations.

(B) THE WORD OF TRUTH AND THE HOLY SPIRIT PRINCIPLES

Since **THE FATHER'S TALK (GOD PRESENT)** is the direct information from **THE FATHER GOD ALMIGHTY HIMSELF,** all positive children of God can be, and will be inspired with this **WORD** because the Word of **THE FATHER GOD, THE CREATOR OF THE UNIVERSE** is a Spiritual Case Study for all souls to improve to have self awareness and a Higherself Consciousness.

When you are inspired and you want to write, make sure that your ideas, principles and concepts base on the Holy Spirit of Truth without changing the ordinance of the **FATHER'S TALK (GOD PRESENT).**

(C) THERE SHALL BE CONSEQUENCES THAT WOULD FOLLOW THOSE WHO USE THE MEANING, THE CONCEPTS AND THE PRINCIPLES OF THE FATHER'S TALK (GOD PRESENT) FOR THE PURPOSES OF MISLEADING

Consequences shall follow those who use the meaning, the

concepts and the principles of **THE FATHER'S TALK (GOD PRESENT)** for the purposes of misleading in any manner.

Any Human-God, human-animal, human-bird or human-fish who has access to **THE FATHER'S TALK (GOD PRESENT)** through any means, be it via books, electronics, audio and otherwise should know that those words are not the words of human beings. The words are transcribed, proofread and accepted by **THE FATHER GOD** as it comes from the **SUPREME STUDIO OF THE ALMIGHTY FATHER GOD HIMSELF,** via **King Solomon Spiritual Library.**

When the signal of the information alerts HRM King Solomon David Jesse Etteh from

THE FATHER through the **COMPREHENSIVE MEMORY OF GOD** in him, at anytime in the day or at night and anywhere, whether on the road or any public place, he will take note of the title of the Revelation Lectures. Sometimes if the location is conducive, lectures can take place immediately. If the location is not conducive, **THE FATHER** fixes the time for the full lecture to take place. Most of the time, some of the lectures take about a week, a month or six months and so on, to deliver when **THE FATHER** brings it back from **HIS SUPREME MEMORY** to HRM King Solomon Etteh.

Take note that the information of **THE FATHER'S TALK (GOD PRESENT)** is not preaching, or the giving of sermons or shared discussion. **THE FATHER** calls it *"LECTURE REVELATION"*, which is a Spiritual Case Study for mankind to improve and have the Higherself Consciousness about himself or herself and their creator.

For that reason, every human being that comes across any of this information of the **FATHER'S TALK (GOD PRESENT)** should treat it with utmost and absolute respect and reverence at all times.

HRM King Solomon David Jesse Etteh is not responsible for **THE FATHER'S TALK (GOD PRESENT)** but **GOD HIMSELF. THE ALMIGHTY FATHER** only uses him as a way through, just like a loud speaker from the radio or television receiver.

For this reason, HRM King Solomon David Jesse Etteh will not be held responsible by anyone who does not understand the contents, the concepts and the principles of **THE FATHER'S TALK (GOD PRESENT)** information in King Solomon Spiritual Library. He will not answer any questions or queries from spirit to soul and the physical truth in connection to the above from the lower mind individuals, persons or groups. However, if you are positive and you have love, you are humble, have patience and are peaceful and you want to know and understand more of any part of **THE FATHER'S TALK (GOD PRESENT); 'You should use fasting and prayer'** and or if anyone has any questions in good faith, he or she is free to write to HRM King Solomon and **THE FATHER** in him will respond. He will not, and there is no response to any questions, queries and anything negative with the craftiness of the evil minds of humankind.

That is why you should first read

THE FATHER GOD with **HIS SUPREME HOLY SPIRIT OF TRUTH** will bless all those who read and accept this information with good faith through the name and blood of our Lord Jesus Christ. Amen.

In the name of our Lord Jesus Christ In the blood of our Lord Jesus Christ Now and forever more, Amen

ESTABLISH MY SPIRITUAL LIBRARY

I THE FATHER GOD ALMIGHTY THE SUPREME WORD OF THE UNIVERSE AM THE SPIRITUAL FOOD TO FEED YOUR SOUL. Therefore, **I** want every family in this world, every home in this world, every office, government offices, monarchies, countries, states, regions, counties, communities, local authorities compound, family homes, everyone everywhere should be collecting published copies of **THE EVERLASTING GOSPEL AND THE FATHER'S TALK (GOD PRESENT)** Lectures Revelations of KING SOLOMON SPIRITUAL LIBRARY should be established physically in your houses. So that everybody should have those RECORDS. Go to read the books regularly. Every family should have this Library **MY INFORMATION CENTRE** for their family members.

Every generation of the particular family could easily go to their family Library of KING SOLOMON SPIRITUAL LIBRARY EVERLASTING GOSPEL and the **FATHER'S TALK (GOD PRESENT) Lectures Revelations** and read the Gospels and Lectures Revelations. Generations upon generations will access their KING SOLOMON SPIRITUAL LIBRARY.

You must all have **THE LIBRARY OF THE FATHER GOD ALMIGHTY** called **KING SOLOMON SPIRITUAL LIBRARY FATHER'S TALK (GOD**

PRESENT) LECTURES REVELATIONS in your homes and offices. The authorities and individuals concerned must see to that. When you establish your branch of KING SOLOMON SPIRITUAL LIBRARY and have Everlasting Gospels and the **FATHER'S TALK (GOD PRESENT)** Lectures Revelations that place is blessed and secured. In the name and Blood of Our Lord Jesus Christ, now and forever more, Amen.

THANK YOU FATHER

"THEUNISAL-SUREME SEACELION"
The Universal Supreme Season Celebration
=========

"THEUNI-SUREME WORA THECRO-THEUNISE"
The Universal Supreme Word Almighty
The Creator Of The Universe
==============

WWW.COME4WORD.COM

THE OFFICIAL SITE FOR
============

EVERLASTING

UNIVERSAL ALL WORD SEASON APPRECIATION CEREMONIAL PROGRAM

==========

THE UNIVERSAL SUPREME

ALL WORD

SEASON

CELEBRATION

(GOD PRESENT)

SOMETHING MORE THAN

'GOLD'

THE HEART OF ALL MEN

IS

WORD

==================

THE WORD IS THE MAKER,
THE SOLE ADMINISTRATOR
AND
THE CREATOR OF THE
UNIVERSE.
THEREFORE, ALL
HUMANKIND ON EARTH
MUST APPRECIATE
THE WORD IN ALL
CAPACITIES FOREVER

=============

FROM EVERY
OA OF AO TO AO OF AO

(1st OCTOBER TO 10th OCTOBER).
YEARLY IS
THE UNIVERSAL SUPREME

ALL WORD

SEASON

CELEBRATION TO
APPRECIATE
THE FATHER GOD
ALMIGHTY

=================

CELEBRATION!
CELEBRATION!!

CELEBRATION!!!

THE

UNIVERSAL SUPREME WORD CELEBRATION OF ALL TIME

======

THE

ALMIGHTY FATHER GOD, THE CREATOR OF ALL THINGS BROTHERHOOD

IKOABASIKOABASIKOABASIKOA BASIKOABA

ORGANISED BY KING SOLOMON SPIRITUAL LIBRARY

======

HRM KING SOLOMON DAVID JESSE ETE

INSPIRATIONAL HEAD

IN THE HONOUR OF THE FATHER GOD THE CREATOR OF THE UNIVERSE THE HOLY SPIRIT OF TRUTH AND THE KING OF KINGS AND THE LORD OF LORDS

==========

THANK YOU FATHER

KING SOLOMON SPIRITUAL LIBRARY

THE GOD ENCYCLOPAEDIA WORD OF INFINITY

==========

King Solomon Spiritual Library,

God Universal Information Centre
FATHER'S TALK (GOD PRESENT)

WITH LOVE

Covered: **This BOOK,** e-book, software or software's, books, website, video, audio, idea or ideas, formula or formulas, manual or instruction manual.

... Hereby gives you a non-exclusive license to use the ... (THIS BOOK).
Some of the word here is coded with the (WORD OF SUPER HOLY AND INTELLIGENCE FATHER GOD ALMIGHTY)

Title, ownership rights, and intellectual property rights in and to the Website, Books, E-book, Audios and Videos, Shops and Store – e-Stores, Fundraisings, Celebrations and the supreme word seasons Celebration formulas and arrangement, Positive Inspiration, HOLY (FATA), FATHER GOD ALMIGHTY POSSESSING SPIRIT in thought, in words and in deed, thinking well, speaking well, hearing well and doing well shall remain in me and in ... The BOOK is protected by international copyright.

**FATHER'S TALK
(GOD PRESENT)**
The message in THE FATHER'S TALK (GOD PRESENT) does not challenge any authority either individuals, groups or governments of any land or even any belief of any form. It is rather challenging the truth that is hidden from mankind. Therefore, any spirit, soul or physical human being who decides to challenge this truth shall have himself or herself to blame.

Key A

Any individual that reads any of THE FATHER'S TALK (GOD PRESENT) with faith; love and acceptance will experience immediate positive change in his or her life from spirit, soul to physical. If he or she accepts the message then he or she will be free from any evil.

Key B: PEACE AND LOVE

If you do not believe the contents of any of THE FATHER'S TALK (GOD PRESENT) it is possible through THE FATHER'S divine love and peace simply to hand over your copy to a friend or somebody else that would like to keep a copy, or signing out from any of the website that connected to THE FATHER'S TALK (GOD PRESENT) KING SOLOMON SPIRITUAL e-LIBRARY without any evil and negative comments and you are blessed and free.

=======

FROM THE DESK OF INSPIRATIONAL HEAD

Fees, Prices and Donations; There is no refund on fees, price or donations since your fees price or donations are used as a charity contribution to do administration work of THE SUPREME WORD, So please kindly read this first before you decide to involves yourself in any of the under mention of HRM King Solomon David Jesse ETE universal Inspirational Businesses of (GOD PRESENT) in cash, kinds and otherwise.

I CAME FROM THE FATHER GOD, WITH THE FATHER GOD, AND BY THE FATHER GOD TO ESTABLISH THE FOLLOWING:

Therefore, all distributors and contributors of THE FATHER'S TALK (GOD PRESENT), The Spiritual Advice, Healing and Counselling on General Live (The Universal Supreme Spiritual General Hospital), New Songs and

Psalms of King David and Solomon, The Word of **GOD** Processing City in Ikot Okwo or e-City online, The Trinity Celebration, "**OUC FUND**", The Universal Bank Account For All Creations, "**ERUFA**" ETE Royal Universal Family, "**THEUNISAL-SUREME SEACELION**" The Universal Supreme Word Season Celebration To Appreciates THE FATHER GOD ALMIGHTY "**THEUNI-SUREME WORA THECRO-THEUNISE**" **The Universal Supreme Word Almighty, THE CREATOR OF THE UNIVERSE** should attach this information to all readers, website visitors, distributors, affiliates person/group, celebrant and celebrations centres, supporters and promoters, members, workers and voluntary workers, Ete royal universal palace committee, governments and many other centres as an agreement. Please kindly know that I am not answering to any physical human except **PEACE, UNITY AND LOVE.**

"THEUNISAL-SUREME WORA THECRO-THEUNISE".

I AM IN THE STAGE OF SUPER HOLY AND INTELLIGENCE FATHER GOD POSITIVE MADNESS OF THE HOLY SPIRIT
   OF TRUTH,
   ENYEN ODUDU ODUDU ODUDU ABASI MI OOO ZIM ZIM ZIM ASSASU, POSITIVE POSITIVE POSITIVE. UKEMEKE AKA IDIOK UNAM.
   Let the peace and blessing of THE HOLY FATHER abide with everybody who corporate with this divine FATHER'S TALK (GOD PRESENT)

THANK YOU FATHER
BY
THE HOLY SPIRIT OF
THE FATHER GOD

THROUGH HIS SERVANT

Senior Christ Servant
HRM King Solomon David Jesse ETE
Brotherhood of the
Cross and STAR
Eteroyal Universal family
Ikot Okwo The Great City of Refuge,
 Ete Community
Ikot Abasi LGA-543001
Akwa Ibom State Nigeria-W/A
Tel. 08036693841
Email: ksslibrary@eteroyalmail.com

=============

READ AT LEAST SEVEN LECTURE'S REVELATIONS BEFORE YOU CAN MAKE ANY COMMENTS

In the Name of Our Lord Jesus Christ, In the Blood of Our Lord Jesus Christ, Now and forever more

Everybody should have access and read at least seven **FATHER'S TALK (GOD PRESENT)** Lecture's Revelations before you can make any comments about it. If you do not go through at least seven **FATHER'S TALK** lectures and you comment you may make mistakes. When you make mistakes your blood will be upon you because you would have taken voluntary evolution to misquote **THE FATHER GOD THE CREATOR OF THE UNIVERSE.** If however, you go through any seven of **THE FATHER'S TALK (GOD PRESENT)** –

one of **THE FATHER'S TALK** stands for one SPIRIT of GOD, which means that **FATHER'S TALK GOD PRESENT** Lectures Revelation are witness by the Seven SPIRITS of GOD, which **I** use as the Seven Church of GOD and Seven days of the Week, Seven spirits of Creations in one Supreme energy of THE FATHER GOD,

THE SPOKEN WORD.

When you read seven **FATHER'S TALK L**ectures then, **I, THE FATHER GOD** will reveal you as positive person.

Then you will have a portion in **ME**. One of **THE FATHER'S TALK** will have a portion in you. Then you would know that this information came from **THE FATHER GOD.** THE FATHER'S TALK (GOD PRESENT) is not a mere talk from a man!

In the Name of Our Lord Jesus Christ, In the Blood of Our Lord Jesus Christ, Now and forever more

INVITATION

THE UNIVERSAL SUPREME ACKNOWLEDGEMENT

'THE ONLY SOURCE AND REMEDY

TO END ALL HUMANITY
PROBLEMS'
Join me to Celebrate;
Acknowledge,
Appreciate and give full
RECOGNITION to
THE UNIVERSAL
SUPREME WORD,
YOUR LIFE FORCE,
THE TOTALITY OF ALL
TOTALITIES
YOUR CREATOR,
THE FATHER GOD
ALMIGHTY,
THE CREATOR OF THE
UNIVERSE

WWW.COME4WORD.COM

Contact EMAIL:
hrmkingsolomon@eteroyalmail.com

THANK YOU FATHER

The title List of some of the
FATHER'S TALK
(GOD PRESENT)

1: THE MANUAL OF THE SPOKEN WORD

2: THE MANUAL OF LIFE

3: INVESTMENT WITH GOD

4: ISO IBOT EDEM IBOT

5: THE CHARACTER OF THE NEW WORLD

6: HELPMANTRANS

7: UNDERSTANDING MY WORD

8: TRUTH, POSITION, POST AND NAME

9: NON STOP BLESSING

23: THE FATHER GOD, GOD, GOD THE FATHER

24: HUSBAND, WIFE AND CHILD

25: GOD AND HIS HARBINGER

26: LIFE EVERLASTING

27: POSSESS

28: MY MIND AND MY PLAN

29: AFTER HEART AND AFTER MIND

30: MY DECLARATION & STAND IN BCS

31: BEYOND THE HOPE OF FAITH

32: MENTAL STAIN

33: THE PRINCIPLE OF SELF HOLD

34: THE MASTERSHIP

35: HIDU-CUM

36: THE UNIVERSAL PARENT

50: THE FORERUNNER

51: A OF A TO Z (FIRST OF ALL)

52: MAN IN THREE CAPACITIES

53: THE TRUE LIFE OF HOLY SPIRIT PERSONIFIED

54: IN-BETWEEN THE FATHER & THE SON

55: DIVINE ARRANGEMENT & AUTHORITY

56: TWENTY FIRST CENTURY IS NOT FOR SATAN

57: THE SUPREME WORD SEASON CELEBRATION

58: THE MAXIMUM DEITY

59: TRANSFORMER TRANSMITTER AND WAVE

60: THE SUPREME FUTURE

84: FATHER GOD FINAL ARRANGEMENT

85: THE LOVERS OF CHRIST

86: I LOVE YOU, I LOVE YOU TOO

87: THE UNIVERSAL SUPREME UPDATE

88: THE SUPREME ALTAR

89: THE SOURCE AND DESTINATION

90: A SON LIKE THE FATHER THE KING OF KINGS A ROOTS FROM HEAVEN (NOT THIS TIME AROUND)

91: THE TRUE WITNESS AND THE TRUE SERVANT

92: THE FINAL ARRANGEMENT

93: A TRUE NIGERIAN MAN AND WOMAN

94: EVERYONE MUST PERSONALLY INVOLVE

104: BIAKPAN OBIO AKPAN ABASI (THE NEW JERUSALEM CITY)

THANK YOU FATHER